The Structure of Art

Also by Jack Burnham:
Beyond Modern Sculpture

THE
STRUCTURE
of ART

by Jack Burnham

ASSISTED BY CHARLES HARPER AND
JUDITH BENJAMIN BURNHAM

George Braziller

NEW YORK

REVISED EDITION

Passages from *The Savage Mind* by Claude Lévi-Strauss quoted with
the permission of The University of Chicago Press; English translation © 1966 by George Weidenfeld and Nicholson Ltd.

Standard Book Number: 0–8076–0596–4, cloth; 0–8076–0595–6, paper
Library of Congress Catalog Card Number: 75–143195

Second Printing
Printed in the United States of America

Design: Selma Ordewer

To my wife, Judith

Acknowledgments

Much of the impetus behind *The Structure of Art* results from my own as well as others' critical examination of my first book, *Beyond Modern Sculpture*. By last year the internal inconsistencies of that book were very much on my mind. And just as vexing is the fact that I believe that many of its theories remain creditable.

Its historical presumptions impelled me to study the writing of Claude Lévi-Strauss with more than casual interest. The first notes and thinking for the present book were undertaken at M.I.T.'s Center for Advanced Visual Studies. For this opportunity I wish to thank the Center and the Graham Foundation of Chicago.

The present book grew out of a dialogue between Charles Harper and myself. In fact Harper had several of the initial insights for this approach to structural analysis; a portion of the research for Chapter Three is his, as are several ideas in the text. For his work and many hours of enthusiastic discussion, Harper has my deepest gratitude.

My wife Judith performed a number of indispensable functions: typing, correspondence, cataloguing, editorial assistance, and generally organizing the million and one details that go into any book. For services done with such good will and perseverance, Judith has my loving appreciation.

I also want to thank Northwestern University for its past and present support of my research. My appreciation goes again to Edward F. Fry for his criticism. Judith B. Tankard deserves special thanks for copy-editing the manuscript. And in closing, I am particularly beholden to Janice Pargh, my editor, and George Braziller for their continued belief in my work.

J.B.

September, 1970

Preface to the Revised Edition

The present volume represents extensive revision of the first edition. After *The Structure of Art* first appeared it became evident to me that the art semiotic contains several more logic modes than I had originally proposed. Many of the analyses in Chapter Three are reworked according to a new semiotic matrix, which I believe is the outer cognitive structure controlling the appreciation of art. Much remains to be learned about the perceptual laws defining the "historical" sequential discernment of art. I hope to write about this in future books.

J.B.

April, 1973

Contents

List of Illustrations

Time Continua and the Esthetic Illusion
  I. Historical-Mythic Structures in Art Through Diachronic-Synchronic Synthesis.
 II. Rise of Historical Consciousness in the Making of Art.
III. Division of Natural and Cultural Terms as Used by Claude Lévi-Strauss and Roland Barthes.
 IV. Division of Natural and Cultural Terms Applied to Art Analysis.
  V. A Metalanguage System as it Applies to Works of Art.

Joseph Albers, *Study for Homage to the Square: Closing,* 1964.

The Structural Analyses
  1. J. M. W. Turner, *Rain, Steam and Speed-Great Western Railroad,* 1844.
  2. Edouard Manet, *Mlle. Victorine in the Costume of an Espada,* 1862.
  3. Claude Monet, *Haystack, Winter, Giverny,* 1891.
  4. Georges Seurat, *Evening, Honfleur,* 1886.
  5. Paul Gauguin, *The Spirit of the Dead Watching,* 1892.
  6. Paul Cézanne, *The Basket of Apples,* 1890–1894.
  7. Pablo Picasso, *Daniel-Henry Kahnweiler,* 1910.
  8. Georges Braque, *Le Courrier,* 1913.
  9. Raymond Duchamp-Villon, *The Great Horse,* 1914.
 10. Wassily Kandinsky, *Black Lines,* 1913.
 11. Marcel Duchamp, *Box in a Suitcase or Valise,* 1941/1942 (1961 edition).
 12. Kasimir Malevich, *Suprematist Composition (Airplane Flying),* 1914.
 13. Piet Mondrian, *Composition 2,* 1922.
 14. Constantin Brancusi, *Leda,* 1920.
 15. Naum Gabo, *Column,* 1923.
 16. Paul Klee, *Dance Monster to my Soft Song!,* 1922.
 17. René Magritte, *Song of Love,* 1948.
 18. Henry Moore, *Reclining Figure, II (Two Parts),* 1960.
 19. Jackson Pollock, *Cathedral,* 1947.
 20. Willem de Kooning, *Woman and Bicycle,* 1952–1953.
 21. Franz Kline, *Mahoning,* 1956.
 22. Jasper Johns, *Painted Bronze,* 1964.
 23. David Smith, *Cubi XXVII,* 1965.
 24. Morris Louis, *Saraband,* 1959.
 25. Frank Stella, *Newstead Abbey,* 1960.

A Key to Text References

Each quotation in the text is followed by date of publication, page number and, where appropriate, author of the passage cited. The full source for each reference can be located in the Bibliography, where authors are listed alphabetically. When more than one work by an author appears in a given year, an *a, b, c,* and so on follows the date of publication to identify the title both in the text and in the Bibliography.

Introduction

Experts and Masters of the Game freely wove the initial theme into unlimited combinations. For a long time one school of players favored the technique of stating side by side, developing in counterpoint, and finally harmoniously combining two hostile themes or ideas, such as law and freedom, individual and community. In such a Game the goal was to develop both themes or theses with complete equality and impartiality, to evolve out of thesis and antithesis the purest possible synthesis. . . . We would scarcely be exaggerating if we ventured to say that for a small circle of genuine Glass Bead Game players the Game was virtually equivalent to worship, although it deliberately eschewed developing any theology of its own.

—HERMANN HESSE
The Glass Bead Game (pp. 40–41)

Over thirty years ago Hermann Hesse realized the profound sense of weariness and irrelevancy which had overtaken the art impulse. He sensed that in the frantic attempts to glamorize and immortalize the products of art, society was unconsciously aware that a way of life was passing from existence. During the Second World War Hesse finished a long allegorical novel on just such a society clinging to its art traditions.

The intelligentsia of Hesse's fictional land of Castalia fashioned a highly venerated Glass Bead Game in which all previous culture is thematically integrated. Yearly tournaments of the Game became the intellectual and spiritual focus of the nation's best minds; one could say that participation in the Game became almost a religious obsession. The Game itself was a matrix for dead art as a kind of esthetic surrogate. Here the best minds of Castalia distilled all aspects of previous high culture into an infinite variety of strategies and structures, which could permit the use of ancient Chinese temple plans alongside the harmonies of late Beethoven quartets. In its ritualistic desire to relive the past, Castalia is simply an allusion to a tradition somewhat like our own.

Hesse's hero and Master of the Game (or Magister Ludi), Joseph Knecht, at first accepts these traditions as a *lingua sacra* or divine language. In time, though, Knecht begins to suspect the inevitability of the Game's disintegration, its utter synthetic quality. He wonders if it were not each intellectual's duty to apply himself to living issues, perhaps even

1

to the danger and vulgarity of politics. *The Glass Bead Game* documents such a painful transition for one man. Knecht ultimately comes to realize that for those who practice art, it remains a "strange and pleasant illusion." The Master of the Game ponders the impossibility of ever experiencing art forms as they were once experienced by those who created them. Speaking of choral church music in the seventeenth century, Knecht remarks: "In those days men's ears heard sounds whose angelic purity cannot be conjured up again by any amount of science or magic. In the same way the Glass Bead Game will not be forgotten, but it will be irrecoverable, and those who study its history, its rise, flourishing, and doom, will sigh and envy us for having been allowed to live in so peaceful, cultivated, and harmonious a world of the mind" (Hesse, pp. 361–62).

In much the same spirit this book, *The Structure of Art,* asks perennial questions: What are the visual arts? How is it that the avant-garde periodically produces strange new images, yet we nevertheless learn to accept them as art? Why did a theory of high art arise in the eighteenth and nineteenth centuries? Why is it that, increasingly, contemporary art seems hermetic and obscure? And finally, what is behind the gradual demise of avant-garde art as a living tradition?

It appears likely that we never perceive the conceptual mechanisms of art because art scholarship, upon which most of our knowledge of art relies, is directed only toward secondary structures. The fact that historical and critical analyses of art are essentially descriptive rather than analytical is of singular importance. Historical research, criticism, and connoisseurship, moreover, can never define art; their real function is to perform elegantly and gratuitously as pendants to the work of art. In other words, they prevent explanation. In elaborate detail historians tell us how to look at and think about art. The most impeccable scholarship, utilizing newly verified documents, voluminous footnotes, and convincing empirical generalizations about the development of the art impulse, only succeeds in further indoctrinating us into the art mystique. There is a perverse condition here. It seems that those who *believe* in art produce scholarship which supports their beliefs, while those who are nominally nonbelievers simply ignore art. In effect, art is predicated on a belief structure which operates under the guise of a continual investigation of art. Thus the more we learn circumstantially about the art historical phenomenon, the more we are convinced that art is essentially unknowable and "spiritual" in substance.

Then there is the paradox, as we mentioned previously, of an eternal avant-garde which in spite of its enormous diversity and originality constantly produces something generally accepted as art. As a rule historians try to develop analytical tools covering the broadest array of art styles, but as innovation further fragments the art impulse, and new and contradictory styles of art arise, historians are forced to adopt a variety of approaches. Not too many critics or scholars seem to be worried by this situation, although they should be. It indicates that all their efforts are directed toward explaining the physical evidences of the art impulse, rather than the conceptual conditions which make art objects possible under vastly different circumstances.

This book is an attempt to bridge the gap between art analysis and the staggering variety of means by which art is expressed. Its premise is simply this: firstly, any successful form of art analysis must use the same techniques to explain all forms of art; secondly, effective art analysis must presuppose that the historical consistency of art (call it esthetics) is due to a highly sophisticated but hidden, logical structure observed without exception by all successful artists; and finally, such a method must apply this logical structure to reveal how and in what particular sense artistic expression changes, while remaining the same.

In the following chapters, a method is employed that meets these requirements by combining the Structural Anthropology of Claude Lévi-Strauss and semiological analysis. Both types of analyses are outgrowths of the school of Structural Linguistics that developed and flourished between 1910 and 1950. Such an approach assumes that the historical notion of art is based on a mythic structure (consequently logical within the confines of the structure), and that art functions as an evolving sign system with the same flexibility in the usage of signs enjoyed by any language.

Structuralism is predicated on the fact that all mythic modes of communication mirror the values and goals of the society using them. Consequently content and technique may be altered in the retelling of a myth, but the myth's underlying logic remains unchanged. In the anthropological investigations of Lévi-Strauss, structure (how a ritual, myth, or totemic system is ordered) mediates between what is physically true and what is hoped for. All mythic forms function conceptually as methods of mediation and transformation. Hence the ideal in art is an essential ingredient for the conceptual formulation of art. The structure of art never attains the Art Ideal—whether this is an ideal of beauty, truth to nature, or some ideological principle; rather, it conceptually incorporates the unobtainable into the making and ordering of the art itself. How this is accomplished is one of the major subjects of this book.

One might reasonably suspect that the structure of art is consistent throughout the history of the art concept, and that its origins lie in prehistoric activities of ritual and sacrifice. This is indicated by various references to the field work of Lévi-Strauss, where the structure of rites and art seem to overlap. However, it is not our intention to survey the entire history of artistic endeavor with the purpose of producing a general theory of art. Beginning with some works by nineteenth-century artists, our aim is to show a logical consistency among representative examples of modernist art. Historians clearly recognize the metaphysical implications of art prior to the modern era, but they are remarkably ingenious in avoiding a confrontation with the metaphysical suppositions of contemporary art. Needless to say, these suppositions increasingly assume a rationalistic form as they approach the present. The reasoning of this book, then, is that if we can uncover the metaphysics underlying recent art, the rest will be mainly a matter of applied scholarship.

It must be emphasized that this study makes no pretense of defining the neural structures that account for artistic creativity. The distinctions between unconscious conceptual categories as they apply to mythic thinking and the mechanisms of thought themselves are very great. These will be touched upon in the next chapter through a discussion of Noam Chomsky's theory of "deep structure" versus "surface structure." Our study is confined to a single example of "surface structure," namely that embodied in the logical relationships shared by every object generally acknowledged as a work of art.

Here it may be helpful to explain the general development of *The Structure of Art*. Chapter One is almost a recapitulation of the author's personal introduction to structural thinking. This is not meant to be a professional critique of the scholars discussed, but rather an elaboration of their ideas insofar as these have relevancy to the ontological problems of art. The section devoted to Claude Lévi-Strauss is particularly important as a conceptual basis for the rest of the study. Possibly, after scanning sections on Ferdinand de Saussure and Roland Barthes, the reader will begin to suspect that the subject of the book is linguistics rather than art. Admittedly these summations are thin treatments of rather difficult subjects. If they seem unnecessarily technical or involved, it is because the ideas are not only complex but probably unfamiliar to the average person interested in art theory.

Nevertheless, the second part of the second chapter is a fairly complete explanation of our approach to structural analysis. The hope is that it is thorough enough to stand by itself. If the reader grasps the techniques presented in these few pages, the rest should follow more readily.

The crux of the book is the structural analyses themselves. Examined closely, they provide a factual demonstration of most of the conclusions of this study. Their purpose is to show how art history and the creation of art are mutually supportive activities, each representing the structural inversion of the other, so that in effect art history is the intellectual justification of the art myth. The analyses also demonstrate how art history, as much as technology, is committed to a series of myth-events or "significant breakthroughs" toward vague and shifting goals. In our time such breakthroughs might include completion of the world's first digital computer at Harvard University (1944) or the first landing on the Moon (July, 1969). Parallels in art might include Picasso's initial cubist composition, *Les Demoiselles d'Avignon* (1907), or Jackson Pollock's first drip painting (1947). It is the intensity of conviction that these events are uniquely influential that determines their historical stature. Intellectually, art history has had more than its share of difficulties. For example, classical art was until this century regarded as the standard measure for all art. But then most conveniently the Viennese art historian Alois Riegl produced the doctrine of *Kunstwollen* (or artistic volition) in order to explain the art impulse in societies which had never experienced classicism or had left it for other stages of artistic development. The implication is that as long as classicism was accepted as an eternal ideal, innovational art was merely divergence from the mean. But what if the mean itself was the impulse toward historical evolution? Implicitly, and never overtly, this has become the rationale of art history.

Needless to say, all the landmarks of such reasoning can be found in a previous book by the author, *Beyond Modern Sculpture: The Effects of Science and Technology on the Sculpture of This Century* (1968), whose assumptions address themselves to a dominant mythology of our time, namely beliefs constructed upon past, present, and future technological achievement. It must be emphasized here that myths are not falsehoods; rather, they are modes of communication and exchange that reflect a set of social values and institutions. The book stresses that science presently has considerably more authority than art—although subsequently the underlying premises of *Beyond Modern Sculpture* have themselves been challenged as mythologies, and thus are open to question. On the whole these premises are not exotic, since they are generally accepted forms of behavior in advanced industrial societies. They include: (a) *Anthropocentrism,* or the belief that the Earth is at the complete disposal of its dominant inhabitant, man; (b) *Functional rationality,* the belief that modern societies operate according to logical principles determined by man; (c) *Messianic technology,* the faith that all problems of mankind can be eradicated through further scientific discoveries; and (d) *The illusion of historical progress,* which presupposes that man is moving toward some predestined or structurally determined plateau of perfection. Today, though, such notions are losing ground. It remains to be seen if science will come up with a tenable set of beliefs (since none of the aforementioned are particularly the result of scientific thinking but are, rather, a popular response to the successes of science), or whether new realizations will be so contradictory as to topple confidence in science itself. Quite possibly one of the eventual uses of Structuralism will be to uncover some of the epistomological assumptions of science. This implies that even the most objective techniques for describing physical reality are more or less reflections of our cognitive habits. If this is so, as it seems to be, where does society turn for its ultimate source of authority and verification of its values? Obviously mythic and metaphysical institutions are becoming less and less adequate. Perhaps Structuralism teaches us the futility of depending upon such absolutes as devices for gaining social cohesion.

I

Search for a Structure

But, whether one deplores or rejoices in the fact, there are still zones in which savage thought, like savage species, is relatively protected. This is the case of art, to which our civilization accords the status of a national park, with all the advantages and inconveniences attending so artificial a formula; and it is particularly the case of so many as yet 'uncleared' sectors of social life, where, through indifference or inability, and most often without our knowing why, primitive thought continues to flourish.

—CLAUDE LÉVI-STRAUSS
The Savage Mind (p. 219)

Esthetic doctrines once proclaimed that art was "beauty," "the search after truth," or "significant form"; what passes for esthetics today—that lingering element which makes art *art*—is no more helpful. Like the patient who repeatedly relocates the cause of his neurosis while being careful never to divulge its underlying origins, redefinition diverts us from the structure of art. And when, as Lévi-Strauss maintains, we do structurally derive an activity—for our culture or for others—we have moved considerably toward eliminating it. Myth as the basis of Western art functions not unlike neurosis: neither depends upon a physical form, but so long as either is believed, it continues to exist.

Our purpose in this chapter is to recapitulate the steps leading toward a structural definition of art. Rather than develop an objective outline, an attempt is made to comment on the ideas of scientists and philosophers as they have contributed to the problems at hand. The thinkers reviewed, Claude Lévi-Strauss, Ferdinand de Saussure, Roland Barthes, Noam Chomsky, and Jean Piaget, are presented not chronologically but logically, or in the order which best enlarges our understanding of art as a mythic and logical form. Eventually, it should be apparent that language is the broadest and most useful form of myth, the mode most likely to survive, and consequently the form most analyzed for its conventions. Precisely because of this, the rules of art are mirrored in the surface structure and deep structure of language.

CLAUDE LÉVI-STRAUSS

Central to Claude Lévi-Strauss's concept of Structural Anthropology is his premise that unconscious mental processes remain fixed for all cultures, "primitive" and literate alike. These impose compatible structures upon the entire range of social activities, though many of these structures remain invisible to untrained observers. Thus all customs in a society fill specific functions and act as supplementary "languages." Brilliant elaboration of this theory has made the Professor of Social Anthropology at the Collège de France one of the most discussed thinkers of the last decade.

Generally, Lévi-Strauss has drawn his methods from a number of sources, including Communication Theory, Hegelian dialectics, and Structural Linguistics. He sees the mind as receiving and transmitting experiences in a coded form which unconsciously adheres to established social conventions. The vehicle for such structures is myth itself. Myths represent collective thought, or what a society thinks about itself and its conditions. And while these stories and conventions appear to be random, haphazard collections, it has been the lifework of Lévi-Strauss to show how they articulate specific ideas about man in relation to his environment. Myths are made logical, according to Lévi-Strauss, because they are resolvable into terms which can be divided into conceptual taxonomies revealing relationships consistent with other myths.

In the introduction to *The Raw and the Cooked* Lévi-Strauss delivers some of his most incisive remarks on contemporary art. Myth, he explains, has no practical function; it shares much of the transcendent objectivity which those closest to art associate with art. But while myth remains an "object," something impermeable and self-contained, it retains the structure of a secondary language. This, he says, is the case with music but not with painting. He observes that colors in painting are not equal to tones in music; colors appear in nature but tones do not, except by accident; thus *color* and *noise* are natural signifying terms, but have no communicative effectiveness by themselves. "In other words, colors exist in painting only because of the prior existence of colored objects and beings; and only through a process of abstraction can they be separated from their natural substrata and treated as elements in an independent system" (1964, p. 19).

The difficulty remains in trying to construct a system of signification on a single level of articulation. Lévi-Strauss insists that this is impossible because the plastic arts rely upon organized conventions in order to be understood as art. Hence art is simultaneously connected to two systems: the first is based on a viewer's capacity to organize sense experiences, and the second is a learned system of plastic values. In a viewer's mind, both modify and supplement one another as complementary aspects of a single system of perception. Actually, as Lévi-Strauss explains in a somewhat roundabout way, the difficulty of making abstract art intelligible is fundamentally semantic, not esthetic. He compares Oriental calligraphic painting to its counterpart in nonfigurative painting. Authentic calligraphic painting defines itself through two mutually dependent terms: language (or ideograms) and painterly expressiveness. Western experiments in Abstract Expressionism, Tachism, and mock calligraphic draftsmanship abandon the first half of signification (language) and thus rely upon the contextual meanings of art history, criticism, and biography as substitutes.

It appears that communication in abstract art depends upon acculturized secondary levels of meaning. Even so, Lévi-Strauss concludes that abstract painting increasingly takes over the function of decoration, as it is incapable of semiotic significance. In a brief passage he defines the unresolved dilemma of modernist art: "Does not this dependence on a different idiom betray a feeling of anxiety that, in the absence of a fairly apportioned code, complex messages may be inadequately received by those people to whom they have, after all, to be addressed? Once a language has been unhinged, it inevitably tends to fall apart, and the fragments that hitherto were a means of reciprocal articulation between nature and culture drift to one side or the other" (1964, p. 25).

As critics have observed, *The Savage Mind* is a poor translation of Lévi-Strauss's French title, *La pensée sauvage*. "The Thinking of Savages" is perhaps better, but even this fails to capture the irony of a thesis which repeatedly indicates that the thought processes of so-called primitive peoples and of members of modern literate cultures are essentially alike in logic and methods of classification. Moreover it is perhaps the particular relationship between event and structure (or act and concept) which accounts for differences between science and magic, the latter being more allied to our conception of art. Here Lévi-Strauss observes that all cultures tend to overestimate the objective quality of their particular modes of thought.

In an introductory chapter, "The Science of the Concrete," Lévi-Strauss makes some very useful observations on the logic of artistic thought. He begins by defining the difference between scientific causality and causality employed by practitioners of sympathetic medicine or magic. Both science and magic demand conceptual order; the order that science imposes upon entities is generally conceived to be systematic and concerned with physical similarities, while that of magic adheres to a form of order which meets "intellectual requirements." More explicitly, magical relationships *are* reasonable and logical because they are believed, and they are believed because they *seem* reasonable. In other words, there is a circularity to magical or mythical thinking which is matched in science by demonstrations of physical cause and effect relationships. Repetition is to magic what verification is to science; repetitions are timeless while verifications only exist in time. Lévi-Strauss stresses that science and magic are both complete systems of thought. Science is not the mature outgrowth of magic; rather, the two are scientific as far as they go, magic being more dependent upon perception and imagination, science extending into purely abstract levels of order.

In regard to art, a most important distinction is made between the *bricoleur* and the engineer. An old French term, the *bricoleur* is a kind of handyman who uses whatever means are available. His significance lies in the fact that his forms or materials have no preordained function; they find their place according to spur of the moment notions and activities. The scientist or engineer gives form to function or meaning, while the *bricoleur* gives meaning to form. *Bricolage* has its counterpart in mythic thought. Unlike the engineer, the mythmaker need not subordinate elements to a strict procedure, source of supplies, or a precise set of objectives. The products of the *bricoleur* all develop from things at hand which can be imaginatively recombined.

Here Lévi-Strauss introduces the fundamental concept of signs. Signs in Structural Linguistics possess the flexibility of being both neutral images and active concepts; the *bricoleur,* or mythmaker, uses signs either way. His use is limited to the fact that most signs already possess certain implications within a mythic structure—signs being materials, colors, shapes, or other qualities which may be freely manipulated, but which all the same represent implicit and recognized associations.

Lévi-Strauss attempts one fundamental distinction between mythical thinking and science. The artist or mythmaker manipulates signs into various new permutations; the fact that they are subjected to novel arrangements alters their powers and potential for future signification. Thus for the artist the color yellow may signify countless emotions, harmonies, or relationships with prior works. When mythic forms such as works of art are subjected to comparison, signs are continually reconstituted so that old means become content for new usages; in Lévi-Strauss's words: "Further, the 'bricoleur' also, and indeed principally, derives his poetry from the fact that he does not confine himself to accomplishment and execution: he 'speaks' not only *with* things, as we have already seen, but also through the medium of things: giving an account of his personality and life by the choices he makes between the limited possibilities" (1962a,

p. 21). Since scientific structures remain outside normal social experience while mythic structures are part of it, scientific knowledge attempts to remain detached from events. Hence Lévi-Strauss sees science and myth as divergent logical methods. Here we must disagree with Lévi-Strauss's proposal that the *bricoleur* "builds up structures by fitting together events, or rather the remains of events, while science, 'in operation' simply by virtue of coming into being, creates its means and results in the form of events, thanks to the structures which it is constantly elaborating and which are its hypotheses and theories" (p. 22). It will be shown in Barthes's Semiology that *events* and *structures* correspond to the two components of a sign group; meaning is thus a consequence of the presence of both. So that the idea of an artist building up structures through events, and the scientist doing the reverse, is methodologically questionable—like which came first, the chicken or the egg? This is an example of Lévi-Strauss's propensity for conceptually separating science and myth, whereas science is probably a more sophisticated mythic form. In situations where any form of social communication becomes sufficiently routinized and sophisticated, mythic explanations of its acts are inevitable. A myth dies when it tries to explain or encompass more than itself.

To gain a broad understanding of how art functions, Lévi-Strauss's discussions of totemism are essential. No other thinker has provided us with a more accurate description of the artistic mind. For in classifying everything in his environment, man unavoidably produces a framework of values which unconsciously extends into the making of art. For primitive man totemism expresses the totality of relationships between culture and nature. As is constantly the case in art, the logic of totemism is a kaleidoscope of images and patterns where "reflections are equivalent to real objects, that is, in which signs assume the status of things signified" (p. 36).

In fact what we refer to as "esthetic choice" has its roots in totemism. Nevertheless, this institution was consistently misunderstood by social scientists from its discovery in the nineteenth century. This misunderstanding stemmed from scientists' fears that seemingly primitive institutions would simply mirror their own conventions of art, religion, and nationalism. The result was a most invidious comparison of totemism to organized religion, parodying both ideas in the process. According to Lévi-Strauss, totemic systems are consistent systems of metaphor that unify the natural environment with society. Totems define rules of behavior reflected in the properties of totemic relationships. Totemism, like art, has no set rules, intrinsic characteristics, or prescribed materials; its function "is to guarantee the convertibility of ideas between different levels of social reality" (p. 76). Thus as a logical system, it allows the user to focus on many objects and conditions, just as the artist does in selecting materials and subject matter.

The fundamental dichotomy expressed in mythic forms is that of Nature and Culture. Culture represents all categories created through or by man: family or tribal members, domestic animals, and artifacts. Entities falling outside the control and domain of man belong to nature. In practice, totemism is simply a means for conceptualizing social relationships. It answers the existential question, "Who am I?" and secondly, "Who are the people around me?" In nature, according to Lévi-Strauss, all species of a given animal look alike and, for man's purposes, *are* alike. Consequently, if man is a species of nature, he and the members of his tribe lack personal identities. Culture is the conceptual means for distinguishing man from nature. In order to differentiate within his own species, primitive man assigns the names of animal species to members of his family or clan. Thus by systematically *associating* members of his group with animal species, he *distinguishes* himself from others in his group and also from other species, though he maintains a special relationship to his own totem. In other words, totemism is a system of homologies; rather than being a form of animism or supernatural kinship with nature, these species-group relationships act as *signs,* and so define separateness between different sets. Contrasts on one plane (various species in nature) are used to define conceptual differences (men in culture) on another. *In art, on the other hand, any entity, natural or cultural, can be naturalized for use as subject.*

On the level of ritual, Lévi-Strauss observes that we must "recognize the system of natural species and that of manufactured objects as two mediating sets which man employs to overcome the opposition between nature and culture and think of them as a whole" (p. 127). This relationship appears to contain all the elementary preconditions for making art.

Art forms are the result of a conceptual reciprocity, the nature of which becomes apparent through Lévi-Strauss's description of marriage exchanges for several North American hunting tribes (pp. 127–28). According to one representative myth, a buffalo falls in love with a girl and desires her in marriage. Symbolically she is without a mother and thus the unnatural product of an all-male tribe. But after consideration the tribal members expediently consent to a marriage. The marriage exchange is mediated by creating a "husband," formed of various tribal artifacts, in the shape of a buffalo. As Lévi-Strauss indicates, the myth, which by itself has no substantial form, is given an added dimension by the assemblage of cultural goods. For the tribe this establishes a visible link between nature and culture, composing a metamorphosis of both. Through the terms of the union, a buffalo (natural), a woman (mediating idea), and a set of objects (manufactured or cultural), the husband represents an imprecise mixture of effects which remain both external to and yet within man's control, and it is this imprecision which remains artistically important. Hence the idea of mediation is central to the act of making art. Moreover, if the principles of totemic classification are universal, then as Lévi-Strauss indicates, they display "a *modus operandi* which can be discerned even behind social structures traditionally defined in a way diametrically opposed to totemism" (p. 129).

Until recently one of the major illusions of Western art, and one of its most valuable supporting myths, was the notion that *laws,* such as Newton's laws of motion for mechanical bodies, existed in some form for the creation of art. One of the characteristics of myths is that they seem to promise rules of order but never deliver them. Undoubtedly conscious knowledge of the rules of art would dispel the illusion of art at once, since these deal with unconscious mechanisms concerning the use of objects, materials, and concepts in mediating reality, namely, in defining the artist's relationships to nature and culture. These relationships, as we shall learn, are only tangentially concerned with physical properties of the art object, that is, its formal content. As proved in the last few decades, art may assume almost any form or be made in any way; the facturing process is not central to the creation of art. Yet the structural significance of the fabricating process vis-à-vis time and the consistency of what is selected is immensely important.

Intrinsically, works of art are devoid of meaning; as signs their meaning lies in becoming a segment of a larger context, that referential system which we elliptically refer to as the history of art. Art's unifying order exists in how the artist reassembles signs within a structure which produces the sense of mediation (art) for him. Linguistically art's effectiveness depends upon its surface "vagueness," which is not meant in the sense of a lack of focus, but rather in the artist's success in shifting our minds from an empirical level of comprehension to the mythic. Writing of totemism Lévi-Strauss notes that "What is significant is not so much the presence —or absence—of this or that level of classification as the existence of a classification with, as it were, an adjustable thread which gives the group adopting it the means of 'focusing' on all planes, from the most abstract to the most concrete, the most cultural to the most natural, without changing its intellectual instrument" (p. 136). Such systems, due to the richness of compounded terms, make unconscious association completely automatic. Thus it should be emphasized that the conceptual structure of science exists in our awareness of it, while the structure of art, by necessity, remains unconscious.

Lévi-Strauss, like many anthropologists, considers totemism to be an institution of synchronic cultures, or cultures lacking a sense of history. In fact, he suggests that all mythic structures collapse outside of synchrony. Nevertheless, there are exceptions: he gives examples of primitive societies which construct their myths on the basis of historical and evolutionary changes (pp. 224–26). Where diachrony prevails Lévi-Strauss claims that historical awareness defeats the possibility of maintaining totemism. History, he insists, threatens cultures which reflect mythic regularity through their sense of timelessness. Such a thesis, however, cannot account for the history of art, which by definition is diachronic but shows evidence of being mythic too. Moreover, Lévi-Strauss is very aware of this inconsistency and deals with it not too satisfactorily (pp. 231–36): "Mythical history thus presents the paradox of being both disjoined from and conjoined with the present. . . . It remains to be shown how the savage mind succeeds not only in overcoming this twofold contradiction, but also in deriving from it the materials of a coherent system in which diachrony, in some sort mastered, collaborates with synchrony without the risk of further conflicts arising between them" (p. 236).

In the chapter "Time Regained," Lévi-Strauss describes the not altogether clear role of *churinga*. These are small, oval-shaped objects made of wood or stone, sometimes engraved. Within the Aranda tribes of central Australia each one of these objects represents the incarnation of a specific ancestor. Placed in remote caves, the churinga are periodically taken out, inspected, polished, greased, and prayed over. For Lévi-Strauss these are comparable to our own archival records, secreted in special institutions, and brought out for state occasions. The churinga, unlike icons, play a part similar to that performed by totemic relationships: they establish differences and connections, in this case between an ancestor and his living descendant possessing the churinga. Thus the churinga, like archives, gain meaning by acting as physical proof of the past; they put us in contact with the myth of history by conjoining two points in time. "For in them alone is the contradiction of a completed past and a present in which it survives, surmounted. Archives are the embodied essence of the event" (p. 242).

One hypothetical issue in esthetics is the seemingly trivial question of whether undetected art forgeries have historical validity. Usually the answer is that they do not, and the reasons most often invoked have to do with stylistic consistency or the utter uniqueness of the artist imitated. But regarded in the context of important records which have been destroyed and replaced with copies, the real reason becomes evident. We accept copies but feel no compulsion to venerate them. A known false work of art cannot mediate between past and present, the diachrony of history and the synchrony of mythic event. Belief in the physical authenticity of the work of art is absolutely essential to myth, since the object is the transubstantiated energy and psyche of the artist it survives. Hence totemism in art not only moves laterally in terms of linking contemporary art forms, but also vertically with relation to past and future events.

In *The Raw and the Cooked* Lévi-Strauss deals with the dualities of myths which are concerned with immortality and its loss. If men are not immune to death, how do they face death and its aftermath? "Is it possible to avert death," he asks, "—that is, prevent men from dying sooner than they want to? And, conversely, is it possible to restore men's youth once they have grown old, or to bring them back to life if they have already died? The solution to the first problem is always formulated in negative terms: do not hear, do not feel, do not touch, do not see, do not taste. . . . The solution to the second problem is always expressed positively: hear, feel, touch, see, taste" (1964, p. 162). As a rule, myths are pragmatic about individual men, but hopeful about the durability of cultural institutions. It seems apparent that dichotomies appearing in myth are essential to the popularization of modern art. For example, the poor and unknown artist who dies at a relatively early age becomes immortal through his work. In life his art is worthless; after death it becomes priceless. While living he is considered insane or at least eccentric; after death his behavior is transformed into prophetic sensitivity or alienation from an insensitive society. Such interpretations are relatively modern and seem to have reached their height in the first part of this century. A minor myth celebrates the prolificacy of aged artists, for example, Rodin, Picasso, and Matisse. Thus myths accommodate all contingencies. Yet the relatively recent popularity of abstract art produces almost absurd contradictions within mythic forms; we experience the phenomena of artists who are rich and immortal at thirty, artists who are disregarded when old, and artists who find their slot in history books at the convenience of dealers. Consistent violations of mythic structure always point to the dissolution of myth itself.

Then there is the scientific credibility of Lévi-Strauss's methods. In the wake of his innovations, it appears inevitable that Lévi-Strauss should have his critics. While possessing respectable Marxist credentials, his position has been attacked as "antihumanist" by the Left in France. In the United States and England the reliability of his enormous ethnological material has been challenged, as have his interpretations. A damaging argument against Structuralism is perhaps this: Those who desire to find structural relationships among very dissimilar materials—by imposing structures—will undoubtedly find them, or anything else sought. Less critically, the very symmetry and elegant simplicity through which Lévi-Strauss reveals underlying meanings is suspect by some anthropologists who have battled with equally intractable data, leaving it in less polished form rather than falsify. But of course even in hard science conceptual *structures* remain the backbone of achievement. The physical sciences assume that all structures impose points of view upon events, and that only their consistency with other events makes them useful. Thus one can only reply that if structures do reappear in a variety of materials with consistency, *they must exist.* For setting chapter outlines of *The Raw and the Cooked* to musical forms, Lévi-Strauss was accused of mixing poetry with science (although he could just as easily be commended for practicing what he believes, namely that myth is the reconciliation of poetry and science). Among Lévi-Strauss's peers, Edmund Leach, head of the English school of Structural Anthropology, was very early one of Lévi-Strauss's most damaging, but fairest, critics. Yet by 1967 Leach felt compelled to write: "it seems to me that anthropologists had good grounds for being thoroughly skeptical about Lévi-Strauss's 'structural analysis of myth' when this technique was first expounded in 1955, but that since the publication of *Le Cru et le cuit* [*The Raw and the Cooked*] in the autumn of 1964 it is possible to quibble only about details. Lévi-Strauss has shown that there *is* such a thing as 'a language of myth,' and he has shown what sort of language it is and how it conveys significance" (Leach, p. xviii).

Our intention is to develop structuralist thinking in a coherent approach to art. The parallel aim of Lévi-Strauss is to provide a logical scheme for mythic institutions. As the anthropologist Mary Douglas observes, not only does he show that the nature of myth and reality are dialectical, but he insists that myth is dialectical in relation to reality. She writes (Leach, p. 57) that "he develops the idea that myth expresses a social dialectic. It states the salient social contradictions, restates them in more and more modified fashion, until in the final statement the contradictions are resolved, or so modified and masked as to be minimized." In a similar manner myth feeds the distinction in our society between objects imbued with transcendent meaning (through the art or religious context) and countless objects produced for everyday use. Nearly a decade ago necessity led sculptors to devise objects, as in Minimal Art, which appeared trivial, but which nevertheless functioned as art. Inevitably, this led to the creation of art without objects. Thus the demise of the transcendent object was accomplished by uncovering the cognitive structure surrounding objects that had been committed to the art context. In such a way myths eventually demythicize themselves.

FERDINAND DE SAUSSURE

The Saussurian principles of Lévi-Strauss's Structural Anthropology are brought out in the publication of his inaugural lecture for the Chair of Social Anthropology at the Collège de France in 1960. In this book (1962b), Lévi-Strauss includes social anthropology as one of the semiological sciences, stating that "Signs and symbols can only function in so far as they belong to systems, regulated by internal laws of implication and exclusion, and the property of a system of signs is to be transformable, in other words, *translatable,* into the language of another system with the aid of permutations" (1967, p. 31). This definition circumscribes the science for which the linguist Ferdinand de Saussure had only tentatively suggested the name Semiology, the study of sign systems within a society.

Saussure's discoveries were pieced together after his death and published under the title, *Course in General Linguistics* (1915). He established the first concrete method to depart from systems of grammar and lexicon for analyzing the materials of speech. Saussure pictures language as being divided into a series of psychological entities called *signs,* each composed of two parts: a *concept* and a *sound-image.* These are transposed into the respective terms *signified* and *signifier* which denote an interconnected whole. The sign has characteristics determined by its context in the line of speech and also by the internal relationship of the signified to the signifier. Signs used in language have to be arbitrary or unfixed in meaning; also, the sound element of the signifier must exist in time.

Saussure notes particularly that language changes only through ordinary unconscious usage and *not* through the interventions of grammarians or logicians, an observation which seems to bear out the axiom: *use defines meaning.* He further separates speech from language: language is speech without sound, all the habits of speech as they can be recorded and studied. Thus the *signifier* is to the *signified* as *speech* is to *language.* Also, within the oppositional categories set up by Lévi-Strauss, signifier and speech are *natural* elements while signified and language are *cultural* elements.

The most dynamic aspect of signs is the ambiguity of their fixed/unfixed and static/temporal nature. Not only do signs suggest opposition, but it is an essential part of their existence. This "inner duality" implies that while language evolves in time, or through time, speech for every user is a fixed convention, a set of communication rules existing outside time. Thus

Saussure denotes static linguistics, or the study of speech through any given time slice, as *synchronic* linguistics, and evolutionary linguistics as *diachronic,* the terms adopted by Lévi-Strauss to specify cultures with mythic structures and those with a sense of their own history.

Saussure makes a working distinction between synchrony and diachrony by comparing speech to chess play. The chessmen and their positions on the board correspond to the juxtaposition of linguistic terms. In speech, like chess, the relative meaning of signs shifts from moment to moment, while the rules of language or chess are fixed. Each move on the board, or segment of speech, only affects the single component involved; but simultaneously the entire context of conversation shifts, just as the chessboard reveals a more or less altered set of opportunities with each move. The distinction that Saussure makes between diachrony and synchrony is that of calculus to simple algebra; diachrony is an infinite succession of synchronic events. The illustration of speech as a chess game should be held in mind, for it will reappear as a metaphor used extensively by Marcel Duchamp.

Again in relation to chess, Saussure brings up the notion of values. Outside the game of chess individual pieces have no value; all value emanates from their rank and position in a given game. He continues: "We see then that in semiological systems like language, where elements hold each other in equilibrium in accordance with fixed rules, the notion of identity blends with that of value and *vice versa"* (Saussure, p. 110). In other words, in a static analysis of linguistical terms all the problems of separating or identifying the "unit, reality, concrete entity, or value" in the terms will always occur. In much the same way the *value* of a work of art cannot be separated from its *concrete reality* in the history of art.

On another level of linguistical opposition, Saussure contrasts the idea of *syntagmatic* units, or word groups, with *associative* (or *systematic*) units. According to Saussure, words in a linear series produce their values vis-à-vis one another through contrast and association. Syntagm is usually "a term [which] acquires its value only because it stands in opposition to everything that precedes or follows it, or to both" (p. 123). Associative relations on the other hand are word units which have grammatical or lexical affinities while possessing no definite order as to the way they appear relative to one another. In the Natural-Cultural dichotomy established by Lévi-Strauss, the syntagm (or unrelated series of oppositional elements) is always natural, while the associative (system or sets of related elements) is always cultural. Thus in language, the logic of mythic structures is always present; syntagmatic and systematic terms are constantly linked to produce signs, which in turn are recombined to produce new meanings. Language, like myth, offers large numbers of interdependent terms which simultaneously modify each other so as to produce shifts in value. The rules of organization for speech are implicit in learning to speak, just as the "rules" for retelling a myth are contingent upon first hearing and believing in the myth.

Because it plays a role in Barthes's Semiology, one last principle of Saussurian analysis should be stated; this is the role of *motivated* and *unmotivated* terms. Motivation implies that a syntagmatic unit may be analyzed culturally, or that a systematic unit may be grouped with associated units as part of a cultural series. Motivated terms account for the illusion that art is timely and logically directed, while, in fact, motivated terms are only half of any work of art. It follows that art that tends toward motivated terms relies on meanings already learned; while art that tends toward unmotivated terms is more "lexicological," that is, expressive by means of signifiers that gain meaning afterward through esthetic ideologies.

ROLAND BARTHES

Surprisingly, the entire trajectory of what is known as Modern Art was defined as early as 1953 in Roland Barthes's *Writing Degree Zero*. This long essay is not so much a critique of the avant-garde as a commentary on the "disintegration of bourgeois consciousness." Barthes cites the relationship between historical awareness and literature feeding upon that consciousness. It is just this tendency toward internal synchronization with the past, a formal completeness, or what Barthes calls "concretion," which ultimately separates literature from its powers of signification. Allowing means to represent themselves becomes the method by which literature achieves Formalism and ultimately rejects it, as literature overextends itself into meaninglessness and ordinary speech. In the same way, hyperconscious Formalism forces art toward blatant assertions of its own "objecthood." As in the craftsmanship of Flaubert, "action" or working methods eventually function as a pendant to style, ultimately becoming its inversion.

Even prior to his introduction to Saussurian analysis, Barthes sensed the distance between contemporary writing and the mythic origins of Classical literature. Classical thinking functions as discourse, a fluid give and take with nature. By contrast modern literature intentionally congeals into stylistic blocks. With Flaubert the labor of writing becomes hyperstyle "in the manner of an art drawing attention to its very artificiality" (1953, p. 65). Forced, by concessions to the history of style, to forego social exchange in the broadest sense (politics), the artist remains bound "to his own formal myths." History overtakes the artist each time the search for a "nonstyle" is successful.

This is early Barthes, a theorist acutely aware of sociohistorical undertones of art ideologies. Barthes is probably the first critic to understand that organized social relationships are in themselves complete language forms. The first steps of such a study, after his introductory *Elements of Semiology* (1964), were made in *Système de la mode* (1967).

Where Saussure postulated that a science of Semiology *includes* language among the conventional modes of social communication, Barthes insists that language must remain as the focus of analysis of any social code; thus all iconic messages have their social equivalents in verbal form (obvious examples for us are art criticism, scholarly analysis, and art history). Barthes proposes that interpretive language, stemming from the signifying system itself, provides a wealth of clues to the hidden social meanings and values behind all such forms of communication. Thus Semiology is a segment of linguistics, a form of secondary linguistics, since it accepts terms, phrases, and concepts on resolution levels too coarse for Structural Linguistics. Moreover the same dichotomic form typifying the efforts of Lévi-Strauss and Saussure is employed. Some of the fundamental terms are related in the following manner (Notice that a sign of *equivalency* rather than a sign of *equality* connects the terms of all the structural equations in this book. A sign of equivalency suggests that connected terms are not mathematically equal, rather that they conceptually correspond to each other):

$$\frac{\text{SIGNIFIER}}{\text{SIGNIFIED}} \backsimeq \frac{\text{speech}}{\text{language}} \backsimeq \frac{\text{image}}{\text{concept}} \backsimeq \frac{\text{form}}{\text{content}}$$

Again signifier falls into the Natural column and signified into the Cultural. The *perceived* in the above sets of terms is the signifier, while its ideational, linguistic counterpart is the signified. Thus the "sign," or set of *image* and *concept,* assumes a dual form:

$$\frac{\text{image}}{\text{concept}} \backsimeq \frac{\text{a mental picture of the object}}{\text{a mental list of the object's}}$$
$$\text{formal qualities}$$

The Natural-Cultural dichotomy can be reduced to terms denoting social equivalents:

$$\frac{\text{NATURAL}}{\text{CULTURAL}} \backsimeq \frac{\text{individual}}{\text{society}} \backsimeq \frac{\text{selection}}{\text{values}} \backsimeq \frac{\text{usage}}{\text{system}}$$

Barthes stresses the contractual nature of language and speech. Since speech is the active, day-to-day use of language, shifts in language occur because of the evolution of speech patterns. Speech on the other hand derives its powers of communication from the unconscious rules of language as they evolve historically. In Barthes's words, "a language is at the same time the product and the instrument of speech: their relationship is therefore a genuinely dialectical one" (1964, p. 16).

In a culture conscious of history, language becomes the anchor or stabilizer of speech. And even though a number of factors contribute to the sense of "great art" and "minor art" in literate cultures, in the art world there is a definite set of relationships ordering the semiological hierarchy:

$$\frac{speech}{language} \; \rightleftharpoons \; \frac{\text{the production of art}}{\text{art criticism, esthetics, and past art}} \; \rightleftharpoons \; \frac{\text{criticism, analysis, and esthetics}}{\text{art history}}$$

In a discussion of Lévi-Strauss's distinction between art and science, the point was made that *event* and *structure* are in opposition, and therefore neither term precedes the other; event is always integral to structure as in:

$$\frac{process}{system} \; \rightleftharpoons \; \frac{event}{structure}$$

As a result, the temporal condition of a sign is always synchronic, reducing all processes and events to ideal points in time. Hence it follows that all signs resist history, functioning outside the passage of time. Signs representing historical events exist as incremental marks on a temporal line. In art history, historians choose events which are then placed hierarchically: the event of a painting < the event of a series of paintings < a period in an artist's development < the artist's entire work < a stylistic era < the era as part of the history of art. History remains the most encompassing sign. This selection process is influenced largely by the ease with which events are nested into the larger schemes of signification.

Barthes stresses that it is virtually impossible for any group to control common language usage. Speech sets it own rules, so that ultimately language is established through existing practice. On the other hand, mass-produced goods constitute sign systems which are thoroughly regulated. The objective though is to make control as anonymous as possible, instilling in the public the illusion that mass-produced goods remain a system largely defined by common usage. Somewhat to the right of ordinary goods is clothing, where individual innovation is recognized, particularly at the level of high fashion. Art, on the other hand, demands full recognition of each innovator. When it is impossible to assign an individual's name and biography to a given art work, even art of accepted quality, the object to some extent suffers from a lack of historical identity.

In practice, the groups that control art are artists's peers, critics, galleries, museum curators, art historians, and major collectors. It is Barthes's feeling that control groups do not destroy the linguistic freedom of a given field, providing there is a certain amount of dialectical play between *usage* and *system.* In contemporary art this situation has been strained as progressively fewer options are left open to the artist. Another dilemma is a growing mutual suspicion between the control groups and the artist. This is the case as artists begin to suspect that rewards from the control groups are in direct proportion to artists' ability to demonstrate continuity within the dialectical scheme of art history.

Barthes makes certain semiological distinctions between the *signified* and the *signifier.* The signified is a concept or mental representation of the "thing." Signifiers are inseparable counterparts of signifieds in forming signs; sounds, objects, images, colors, gestures, and other purely sensory phenomena are lexical elements which signify. Signifiers are separated within a semiological system according to the part they perform at a given level.

Signifier and signified form a single sign, hence deriving meaning through juxtaposition with other signs. Barthes raises the important issue of *motivated* and *unmotivated* signs. Within language he cites the occurrences of onomatopoeia as a natural, but still unclear, form of motivation. He is less specific about the role of motivation in semiological systems outside language. Motivated signs consist of analogies between signifier and signified where parts of a sign seem to have an unlearned or intrinsically logical relation to each other. Barthes is somewhat unsure what constitutes motivation in language when it may appear on some semantic levels but not on others. Obviously there are many signs which are only "relatively" motivated, and Barthes is quite right when he suggests that such impure systems will probably be found in art and other iconographical systems.

The importance to art of a sign with multiple signifieds is considerable. For example the color yellow in a painting by Van Gogh may be purely contextual (compositional and thus unmotivated) on one level, related to the concept of a sunflower on another, and also relatively motivated through biographical knowledge of Van Gogh's passionate disposition. This, in fact, is a modern example of totemism. Here through means of a metaphorical "adjustable thread," a group of people may focus on a number of planes of association "from the most abstract to the most concrete, the most cultural to the most natural, without changing its intellectual instrument" (1962a, p. 136). Thus Van Gogh compels motivated and unmotivated aspects of a single signifier to function as several different signs. Cognitive tension results when Van Gogh stresses the unmotivated levels of such signifiers by emphasizing the purely formal character of yellow juxtaposed to violet or brown.

Barthes makes the observation that the tendency within all semiological systems is "to naturalize the unmotivated and to intellectualize the motivated [that is to say, to culturalize it]" (1964, p. 54). Saussure considered all linguistic signs to be unmotivated because of their essential arbitrary nature; and within the realm of language there is no reason to take exception to this rule. The problem of motivated signs is, however, highly relevant to art. *All* mimetic conventions are motivated since there are isomorphic characteristics between representational lines, colors, and shapes and their models in the real world. Barthes's statement alludes to the pressures causing deterioration within historical semiotic systems.

"To naturalize the unmotivated" means to depend more and more upon the Gestalt relations found within pictorial elements—detaching them from their content, if any. The significance of the other term, *"to intellectualize the motivated,"* may be less obvious at first glance. Until the last eighty years the content of art rarely needed a supplementary explanation since, in fact, the art explained the content. But as art has evolved, content has become the vehicle by which the artist elaborates upon his techniques and formal devices. Thus, as a rule, motivated signs are culturally preestablished, while unmotivated signs are imposed for esthetic reasons, the second system always trying to achieve the legitimacy of the first. This intellectualization of motivated signs ultimately concludes in metalanguage statements which bring the illusion of content to art confined to unmotivated signs, i.e., nonobjective art.

Equally significant is the relationship of motivated and unmotivated signs to the history of art. A primary idea, and one which will be developed in subsequent chapters, is that *"systematizing" the lexicon of signifiers while "expressing" the grammar of signifieds provides both the illusion of constancy and of evolution in art.* In other words, motivated signs give us associational references to contemporary ideas and images which are always transformed into art. This provides a portion of the *plane of content* for some but not all nonobjective styles of art. Art is equally the result of the Saussurian *plane of expression,* or the artists' ability to organize subject matter into a personal handwriting. Where this is destroyed or reduced to ambiguous dialectical oppositions, the ability to "think art" is soon lost. (With this in mind, it becomes apparent that the author's book *Beyond Modern Sculpture* is primarily a study of motivated signs found in sculpture. The book defines chronological parallels between science and art as responsible for shifts in visual expression. Chronologically there are some strong correspondences between artistic and scientific innovation, but these are coincidental not causal relationships.)

Syntagmatic and *systematic* relationships in linguistics serve as the two essential axes for semiological analyses. Syntagmatic relationships have an affinity with the juxtaposed ordering of very different combinations of words, as in speech; while systematic relations are concerned with orderly relationships among words and their syntax, as in language. Barthes emphasizes that the syntagm cannot proceed, that is, be uncovered, without concurrent disclosure of terms from the systematic plane. He is aware that "iconic syntagms," such as contained in photographs, are difficult to identify. Barthes speculates that captions on photographs provide the discontinuity necessary for separation. But it seems, apart from Barthes's remarks, that art, through titles, criticism, and stylistics, provides at least some of the necessary linguistic relationships for separating terms in analyses.

Syntagmatic units are defined by the *commutation test,* which entails substituting new expressions on the plane of signifiers and observing if they bring about corresponding changes in their counterparts on the plane of signifieds. The goal, as Barthes observes, is to create a different homology or a substituted set of structural relationships. If substitutions produce a new set of terms among the signifieds, then a part of a system's syntagmatic structure has been defined. As units of the syntagm are pieced together, they reveal the systematic terms of a system.

An important aspect of the syntagmatic plane is its relation to "certain aleatory factors." In other words, there are statistical probabilities—generated by random events—which ensure that given means of expression are "saturated" by given forms of content. Linguists call this phenomenon *catalysis,* and it refers to the exhaustion of certain signifiers through their connection with all related signifieds. In language such boundaries are both useful and normal. Speech is never exhausted, while the experimental use of language in literature may approach exhaustion. However, there are more serious problems within avant-garde art. Exhaustion through catalysis is the impetus by which art constantly regenerates itself. As forms of expression (the syntagm) are used up, worn out from overuse, art becomes dependent upon fewer systematic relationships. Thus as less and less is permissible in avant-garde art, the artist is compelled to employ expressive terms without having them mean anything in the structural articulation of his art. In precisely this way the idea of randomness is incorporated into an artist's work as an expressive feature. Thus, the artist is signifying that he is no longer concerned with a particular choice system.

Most early formal innovation came as a consequence of disrupting the "speech" character of art (the object perceived before analysis), so that system and syntagm failed to follow an expected sequence. According to Barthes, this is a major source of creativity, "as if perhaps there were here a junction between the field of aesthetics and the defections from the semantic system. The chief transgression is obviously the extension of a paradigm on to the syntagmatic plane . . . this is what would happen, broadly speaking, if one attempted to elaborate a discourse by putting one after the other all the terms of the same declension" (1964, p. 86). Such "transgressions" are extremely revealing. They imply two things: first, that signifiers are progressively more detached from systematization, and second, that signifieds lose their meaning and become detached from the traditional art context. On the planes of syntagm-system, syntagms gradually lose their legibility and systems are reduced to increasingly inflexible sets of rules. So every significant innovation in contemporary art demands not only a cultural readjustment of the syntagm-system to a degree where "speech" or normalized art is possible again, but also a reevaluation of the mutual interaction between syntagm and system. Hence the ease of "speech" in a semiological system is, inherently, the lack of strain and artificiality existing between the two opposing planes.

One of the most useful concepts in Semiology is that of staggered systems. Analysis of modernist art would be impossible without it. Staggered systems operate on two or more levels. All first level signs are what Barthes refers to as the "Real System," or that set of activities and art propositions which are combined to form the immediate substance of the work of art. A second level is composed of the first level reduced to the object and its semiological meaning.

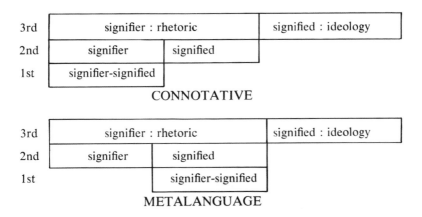

3rd	signifier : rhetoric		signified : ideology
2nd	signifier	signified	
1st	signifier-signified		

CONNOTATIVE

3rd	signifier : rhetoric		signified : ideology
2nd	signifier	signified	
1st		signifier-signified	

METALANGUAGE

In the first example of a staggered system (connotative) the primary level is where a sign (signifier and signified) is used as the plane of expression (signifier) for a second system. This is called a connotative system because the first level is usually signified by language, which then connotes the second level. On the first level, the signifier is the visual image of a printed text, while the signified is the meaning of the text. The second level signified in such a structure is usually the "content" or idea which provides a frame of reference for the second-level signifier, the art object itself. The second level of a connotative system connotes the third level whose signifier thus functions as a language-object for examining the lower levels of the system. The opposite of a connotative system is a metalanguage, a two-level system whose plane of content or signified is in itself a semiotic system. All forms of nonobjective art are metalanguages, while the ready-made and some Conceptual Art are connotative systems. For nonobjective art, "painterly expressiveness" and formal innovation can serve as content for a second-level system of signification; consequently metalanguages in art are the expression of an art activity (cognitive and/or physical) as a proposition about art; the personal circumstances, gestures, and emotive intentions behind a painting become its *raison d'être*. As denoted meaning, this level of signification may be raised to a third level of connotated signification through language, that is, criticism or an art text. Here the motivating esthetic behind a style or movement is encapsulated in writings which in turn are open to examination as a signifier.

In either connotative systems or metalanguages, structure may serve as expression or content of a still higher system. This is a repeatable process embodying the historical-empirical principle of transcendency which is the basis of every system of signification. Potentially every semiological system can be incorporated into a new system. All revolutionary scientific paradigms do precisely this. But in art, this capping process assumes a different form. For example, old media may be incorporated into new media; form becomes content, as is the case with Pop Art and particularly Roy Lichtenstein. Similarly, all new myths build on the fragments of discarded mythologies. Marshall McLuhan and Lévi-Strauss have both commented on this process. The second method of capping works of art results when new methods are employed to analyze art theory itself—the present study is just such an example.

Barthes writes of the necessary limitations (both breadth of material and point of view) which must be imposed upon the body of work (or *corpus*) in any semiological investigation. Such a warning, while important, is not particularly relevant or useful to this study. Barthes refers to the diachronic condition of materials created over periods of time. Obviously, approaching an historical progression of art objects synchronically is not sound. But it is our assumption that any structural analysis of art presupposes that semiological systems are essentially mythic structures which *reveal* their synchronic bases through historical juxtapositions of materials. The important thing is to uncover differences and similarities in art works spanning substantial periods of time, or, in other words, to show, as in the case of myth, that art "evolves" without really changing. This is in contradiction to the semiological investigations made by Barthes to date, since a major emphasis in his studies is that semiological systems must cover the range of signs used in a system for a given point in time. He thinks that the problems of diachrony present sufficient barriers to any meaningful study of historical change. On the other hand, avant-garde art of the past one hundred years *presumes* semiotic instability as a norm. Most languages and sign systems, however, function in daily life as if they were completely stable and impervious to change. As Saussure indicated, this is the "invisible" quality of speech. On the other hand, we propose a study of the *signification of change,* that is, the historical rejection of signs within a structurally consistent system, nominally referred to as modernist art.

This represents something substantially different from the text analyses of fashion magazines developed by Barthes in his *Système de la mode* (1967). In his investigation Barthes separates the language and dynamics of the fashion world from that of the daily wearing of clothing. He demonstrates that the terminology used by fashion magazines is to an overwhelming degree codified by relatively stable conventions and influences, so that, in fact, a "language of fashion" is not only evident but predictable (the same is obviously true of art magazines). Barthes separates sociological investigation of fashion, that is, the cycle of style through mass distribution, from that of the diffusion of a stylistic "image" or *haute couture.* The last he sees as a central concern of Semiology, embodying descriptions of intelligence, sensibility, direction, and opinion within society's tastemaking strata.

NOAM CHOMSKY

It would be well for us to consider the capabilities and limitations of Semiology. During the last fifteen years several new linguistic techniques have rendered structural analysis a somewhat dated method in linguistics. These include the theory of "generative grammar" and of a universal substructure pioneered by Noam Chomsky. In clinical psychology Chomsky is recognized for his attacks on contemporary Behaviorism, the linguist's contention being that learning and mental behavior are too rich and varied to be explained by stimulus-response patterns. He insists that a workable psychology must include "a notion of competence," or some theory which accounts for new learning and potential capabilities. In other words, given our vast inventory of behavioral traits, habits, and built-in responses to particular situations, how do we use speech creatively or adapt to new experiences? Both presuppose the modification of already acquired habits. And it is here, Chomsky claims, that present behavioral theory lacks the necessary subtlety to account for open-ended behavior.

Chomsky's book *Language and Mind* (1968) credits Saussure with developing the analytical techniques of *segmentation* and *classification,* or the signifier-signified and syntagm-system divisions previously reviewed. For Saussure these gave a complete picture of structure as it defines language. Nevertheless Chomsky demonstrates (as Wittgenstein did so elegantly in philosophy) how devoid of philosophical penetration Structuralism really is. It lacks in his estimation the ability to disclose or derive multiple propositions in a sentence. Saussure himself recognized such a limitation, but preferred to see linguistical ambiguity as a relatively insignificant aspect of speech, thus a phenomenon which occurs outside of language proper. Chomsky regards Saussurian analysis and all subsequent structural analyses as "surface structure" investigation, while the actual operations of the mind produce mechanisms of "deep structure" based on logically generative principles ensuring creative use of language. He praises Saussure, however, for recognizing a need for future methods.

Chomsky minimizes Lévi-Strauss's *The Savage Mind* for essentially the same reasons. In terms of understanding human thought processes, he claims that it reveals little, merely that primitive peoples also possess the ability to classify (fortunately that is hardly the point of the book). However he gives Lévi-Strauss, N. Troubetzkoy, R. Jakobson, and other anthropologists credit for recognizing the social implications of structural analysis: "The achievement of structuralist phonology was to show that the phonological rules of a great variety of languages apply to classes of elements that can be simply characterized in terms of these features; that historical change affects such classes in a uniform way; and that the organization of features plays a basic role in the use and acquisition of language" (Chomsky, p. 65).

Chomsky further observes that the "real richness of phonological systems lies not in the structural patterns of phonemes but rather in the intricate systems of rules by which these patterns are formed, modified, and elaborated. The structural patterns that arise at various stages of derivation are a kind of *epiphenomenon*" (p. 65, italics added). True, early structuralism never probed the underlying "kernel structures" of sentence formation as Chomsky and his colleagues have done. Sentence construction with its knotty issues of ambiguity, ellipsis, complexity, and interrogation were areas that the structuralists preferred to leave to grammarians. But the semiotic structure for both linguistic and iconic systems does provide a set of relationships encompassing the syntactical problems described by Chomsky. If there is a strict correspondence between linguistic and iconic signs, then one must ask the following question: What mode of logic adequately represents the needs of both language and art?

JEAN PIAGET

The relationship between physical activity and growth of perceptual awareness is an essential aspect of the Swiss psychologist Jean Piaget's investigations of cognitive development. It would be safe to say that children's progressive understanding of causality stems from the fact that bodily actions and surrounding objects are inseparably a part of each other. Generally Piaget believes, as the phenomenologist Merleau-Ponty did, that descriptions of the world can never be separated from man's activities in the world; in fact, they are reciprocally related.

It has already been suggested that modern art is the successive discarding of one signifying element after another in the search for significantly "new" art. Or inversely, modern art depends upon the ability of an artist to create new work by resystematizing syntagmatic elements or by dropping unessential systematizing forms altogether. What will become evident in the analyses to come is that *the rejection of systematizing forms in modern art is approximately inverse to the way children learn to systematize perception of the world.*

According to Piaget, the Bourbaki group in France has reduced all mathematics to three independent types: algebraic structure, order structure, and topology (1970, p. 24). As for development of spatial awareness in children, Piaget finds that early modes of perception are essentially topological, having to do with proximity, separation, surface order, and enclosure. These appear before a child can grasp the geometric form of an object and long before a child is capable of intellectually organizing the parts of an object. Thus there is a real separation between perception and representation. Visual realism or representation results from learning projective and metric axioms for ordering the constancy of objects relative to a point of view, a process not operative until children reach the age of eight or nine. Perception, on the other hand, begins at birth with a child's awareness of the nearness of objects. As a child's topological awareness to his surroundings develops, it begins to conflict with less elementary forms of geometric perception, that is, Euclidian metric geometry and later projective geometry. Of course these geometries were developed prior to topology, but topology remains their theoretical basis. So in fact, while topology remains the most sophisticated form of geometry and one not discovered until the nineteenth century, perceptually and intellectually it represents the mechanisms of spatial organization first employed by children.

According to a theory put forth in *Beyond Modern Sculpture,* the application of different types of mathematics in formalist sculpture follows the approximate order of their historical discovery (pp. 132–48). While the influences of Euclidian geometry, projective geometry, analytical geometry, topology, and number theory seem to apply to nonobjective sculpture, in that order, Piaget's findings would seem to imply that their usage in sculpture has nothing to do with the fact that they recapitulate their sequence of discovery. The most encompassing and sophisticated mathematical systems most recently discovered are precisely the ones first used by children to provide global experiences of their surroundings. So the sign systems devised in Renaissance art through the use of Euclidian metric geometry and projective geometry are in fact the most synthetic and intellectual and those learned last by children. Hence art has proceeded in the last century from metric proportionment and perspective toward intuitions of proximity and fusion. Semiologically this means that modern art has gravitated from complex arrays of terms to very elementary means of signification.

It is stated that "The more analytic perception becomes, the more marked is the relationship of separation" (Piaget and Inhelder, p. 7). Pictorial illusionism creates the most levels of separation through signs, that is, aerial and mechanical perspective, size constancy, shading, and local color. *Separation* is thus the series of learned systems that increases with growth in reasoning, while the early sense of proximity to objects decreases with age. Gradually "the subject begins to distinguish his own movements from those of the object. Here are found the beginnings of reversibility in movements, and of searching for objects when they disappear. It is in terms of this grouping of movements, and the permanence attributed to the object, that the latter acquires fixed dimensions and its size is estimated more or less correctly, regardless of whether it is near or distant" (p. 11). Through such descriptions we recognize the behavioral characteristics identified with Minimal Art; not surprisingly they are the habits of perception used by infants. At a later stage in development, children begin to draw not what they see, but rather of what they *think* an object or scene consists; psychologists refer to this process as "intellectual realism." Paul Klee and Jean Dubuffet have employed it with great insight as a mode of expression preferable to "visual realism."

Moreover, concepts of coordinates and horizontal-vertical relationships are only learned by the age of eight or nine. Such systems, Piaget insists, are extremely complicated and unnecessary in the child's early methods of orientation. So when Mondrian reduced the structure of the external world to a system of horizontal and vertical black lines, he was not reducing perception to its essential limits but rather to its most compatible form vis-à-vis the format of the picture plane.

In a sense avant-garde art is the process of unlearning all conscious forms of adult perceptual knowledge—certainly not a new conclusion. But now it becomes particularly cogent in the light of Piaget's attempts to construct a "genetic epistomology," or a theory which accounts for development in the human being of successively more complex levels of intellectual and visual reasoning. As is true of Chomsky's "generative grammar," Piaget rejects any psychology which would account for learning as some kind of programmed or predetermined pattern: "By contrast, for the genetic epistomologist, knowledge results from continuous construction, since in each act of understanding, some degree of invention is involved; in development, the passage from one stage to the next is always characterized by the formation of new structures which did not exist before, either in the external world or in the subject's mind" (1970, p. 77). By the same token, if one were to relate semiotic systems to Piaget's genetic epistemology, it could be said that sign systems seem to evolve in complexity and abstractness directly in proportion to their social usefulness. Art has accomplished the reverse; in losing semiotic complexity it has lost its cohesiveness. Yet ironically avant-garde art has achieved this by regressing from a secondary, abstract form of spatial organization (pictorial illusionism) toward a much broader and more fundamental basis (the three structures found in all mathematical and operational thinking). Thus it appears that not only are conscious mythologies sign systems which have lost their powers of signification, but in the case of art this loss is biologically systematic, recapitulating the stages toward a child's earliest means of perception.

II

Time Continua and the Esthetic Illusion

Alice sighed wearily. "I think you might do something better with the time," she said, "than wasting it in asking riddles that have no answers."

"If you knew Time as well as I do," said the Hatter, "you wouldn't talk about wasting it. It's him."

"I don't know what you mean," said Alice.

"Of course you don't!" the Hatter said, tossing his head contemptuously. "I dare say you never spoke to Time!"

"Perhaps not," Alice cautiously replied; "but I know I have to beat time when I learn music."

"Ah! That accounts for it," said the Hatter. "He won't stand beating. Now, if you only kept on good terms with him, he'd do almost anything you like with the clock."

—LEWIS CARROLL
Alice's Adventures in Wonderland

ART HISTORY AS A MYTHIC FORM

Historically art has been in the position of either being considered inferior to nature or of improving upon nature's deficiencies. In the words of the art historian Erwin Panofsky, "Understood as copies of the sensory world, works of art are divested of a more elevated spiritual or, if you will, symbolic meaning; understood as revelations of Ideas, they are divested of the timeless validity and self-sufficiency which properly belongs to them" (Panofsky, p. 32). We sense in the historian's insight the perpetual irresolution of the art sensibility, that indecision which has led to constant reevaluation of the ideal in art. In a culture which has sought scientific causal justification for every conceivable phenomenon, it is not surprising that the Art Ideal should remain so insecure. For as Lévi-Strauss repeatedly insists, it is the *differences between relationships* which produce the totemic bond. Art can no more copy nature than it can generate ideas; its efficacy is in conjoining permissible cultural and natural phenomena through the agency of the artist.

That pinnacle of artistic achievement, the Early Renaissance, provides us with some of the first nonmetaphysical descriptions of beauty. These assume the guise of proscribed harmonic relationships between the elements of painting, sculpture, or architecture. For Panofsky this was one of the first steps in shaping the "autonomy of esthetic experience." Gradually through this autonomy, ideas of imitation, beauty, nobility, and even harmony have been sacrificed, or shown to be unnecessary to perpetuate the Art Ideal. Yet if a perfectly balanced Nature-Culture mediation is the objective of myth, it is not so difficult to understand why Renaissance historians find satisfaction in the liaison of "scientific rules" and convincingly depicted natural forms. Myth strives for an internal and external consistency. If subsequently that consistency is disturbed it can assume an optimum point in history where that equilibrium is apparently achieved.

Mannerist art destroyed the ordered spaces and serene subject matter of the Renaissance, and in so doing it revealed all the internal contradictions that surface periodically in art. Mannerism's concurrent relaxation and pedantry generated a conscious tension in which normal working procedures were first challenged. Previously, art theory had merely commented upon procedures for the production of art; toward the end of the sixteenth century theory became speculation as to whether rules were even possible.

By the middle of the seventeenth century, Classicism appeared as the most effective means of combating artistic "degeneracy." To be sure, classicist art theory was a philosophical sanctuary that avoided the problems of the day, that is, Mannerism and naturalism. It proposed to model itself on a classical past that may or may not have existed, more likely the latter. The origins of Classicism are neither metaphysical nor naturalistic, but a reinterpretation of the Renaissance notion of the Art Ideal, which called for the "purification" of subject matter through the mind of the artist and of the beholder. Programmatically, Classicism rescued floundering art theory by tying it to antiquity and insisting upon the superiority of art to nature. Panofsky labels this reintroduction of idealism "a normative, 'law-giving' aesthetics." He also realizes that these adjustments have their counterparts in modern times: "For quite consistently, alongside modern Impressionism there was an art theory that tried to establish on the one hand the physiology of artistic 'vision,' on the other the psychology of artistic 'thinking.' And Expressionism—in more than one respect relating to Mannerism—was accompanied by a peculiar kind of speculation that . . . actually led back to the tracks followed by the art theorists of the late sixteenth century: the tracks of a metaphysics of art that seeks to derive the phenomenon of artistic creativity from the suprasensory and absolute. . ." (pp. 110–11).

Thus the art myth always seeks for itself the most authoritative form of verification; in the seventeenth century normative esthetics was in part founded upon previous philological and archaeological discoveries—by the twentieth century its roots included psychology and optical physiology. Consequently "laws of art" only become manifest when the semiotics of art are no longer supported scientifically. Myth's goal is to provide a "normative" basis for belief, thus Formalism serves the twentieth century as Classicism did the seventeenth century.

Eighty years ago art historians began to concede the collapse of classical esthetics; for artists the failure of Classicism had long been a working assumption. The pathos of the Romantic upheaval rested on the tension between the possibility of creativity and the obvious materiality of art objects. Hence the Romantic dilemma could be summed up by a single question: are esthetic beliefs workable in an age whose goal is to explain all phenomena deterministically, consequently at a time when belief in the transcendency of the art impulse is at its lowest ebb? Esthetics of the 1890's began with a new idealism that substituted subjective for objective valuation. As cited earlier, the art historian Alois Riegl expressed this in the principle of *Kunstwollen,* that power embodied in a culture to propagate new artistic sensibilities. Certainly this seemed to be an irreducible demand upon art if it were to survive as an idea. So, gradually the techniques of art analysis were seen to fuse with artistic intentionality: Riegl's "will-to-form."

Its counterpart, or intellectual justification, lay in Conrad Fiedler's doctrine of "pure visibility," a forerunner of Formalism at the end of the nineteenth century. Fiedler justified his reduction of art to formal knowledge on the basis that subjective responses to art should be identified with the expressiveness of the artist, not the viewer; this he proposed as a hard-headed alternative to esthetic idealism.

Theoretical acceptance of artistic volition and "pure visibility" was made possible by the psychologist Theodor Lipps and the art historian Wilhelm Worringer. At a time when modernist art was beginning to gain public recognition, Worringer published his doctoral dissertation, *Abstraction and Empathy* (1910). Using Lipps's psychology of art he wrote: "To enjoy esthetically means to enjoy myself in a sensuous object diverse of myself, to empathise myself into it" (Worringer, p. 5). Through empathy the intentions of the artist are recognized and received, if only with the aid of a verbal ideology, as in the case of abstract or nonobjective art. Evidently this emotional identification with an object is the same intellectual capacity found in people who experience the powers of totemic objects. Such artifacts are designed to signify relations both materially within and outside the object. Moreover the traditional means for ensuring empathetic responses had up to then been through realism, or what Worringer referred to as "organic art." As a prophet of modern art, Worringer's contribution was to cite the geometric, structural, and decorative arts of the past as legitimate objects for empathetic response. Thus Worringer cleared the way historically for justification of contemporary art or, as Lévi-Strauss would say, an art with *signifiers* but few or only ideological *signifieds*.

Such theoretical underpinnings provided a needed response to nineteenth-century rationalist doubt. The "de-organicisation and denial of life" by science no longer threatened the transcendent art impulse—or so Worringer believed. Instead art's "entirely new psychic function" focused on the ability of the viewer to identify with abstract intentionality. Worringer concludes that "The old art [academic remnants of Classicism] had been a joyless impulse to self-preservation; now, after its transcendental volition had been taken over and calmed by the scientific striving after knowledge, the realm of art seceded from the realm of science" (Worringer, p. 135). Subsequent tendencies in art, of course, have cast doubt on the historian's hopes. Real escape from scientific criticism means adapting art to a plausible mythic form, one that would be consistent with scientific thinking.

Heinrich Wölfflin is best remembered for consolidation of formal analysis. He viewed composition as one of the prime sources of esthetic delectation, in which form, line, color, contrast, texture, and arrangement were considered the proper elements for investigating the work of art as an abstract entity. Although Wölfflin thought exclusively of representational (what he terms "organic") art, formal analysis had already begun to be applied to abstract art. (As early as 1890 there are the observations of various Symbolist critics, the most famous being Maurice Denis's assertion that a painting was "essentially a flat surface to be covered with colors arranged in a certain order.") Through the anthropomorphic metaphor and Wölfflin's notion that the human body remains the archetypal subject of art, Formalist criticism and analysis evolved. The primacy of the human form for these writers seems to have been coupled with an adaptation of Gestalt psychology. The organistic basis of the Gestalt school, with its reliance on part-to-whole relationships, nicely satisfied the desires of many art lovers to interpret works of art as didactical organisms, systematically organized along the same terms as the human eye's perceptual capability. Such an outlook was gradually strengthened as diverse talents (such as Wassily Kandinsky, Kasimir Malevich, Piet Mondrian, and Paul Klee) implied a quasi-organic sovereignty for their own art. Didactic organicism, first tied to subject matter and later to the organization of composition through perception, remains the substratum of formalist theory.

Formalism via the organic metaphor accounts for most of the "painterly" and biotic abstraction of the last sixty years. More recently, Pop Art, Optical Art, Minimal Art, Process Art, and Outdoor Environmentalism have defied the esthetic canons set up by Formalism. As a rule, all normalizing esthetics attempt to confine art to boundaries which it deems reasonable, thus accounting for Clement Greenberg's pejorative term "novelty art." Yet it was Bernard Berenson who first applied the term to the pitfalls of esthetic taste: "Novelty, otherness, then consists in the easy, but not too easy, satisfaction given to the cognitive faculties when these throw themselves upon an object after exhausting a prior one. It is so full of craving, so lustful, that it is no better judge of the artistic qualities of the object procuring this satisfaction than the physiological or chemical affection known as being-in-love is a judge of the moral character of its object" (Berenson, p. 153). The epithet "novelty," then, is a double-edged weapon; its use as a form of condemnation obscures innovation by seeking to isolate artistic superficiality.

Consequently Formalism itself is an intellectual justification containing many artistic substyles. As a mythic form its deterioration began when sufficient numbers of artists sensed that its premises had been exhausted. In a memorable article, the art historian Michael Fried attacked Minimalist artists for practicing what they claimed to have rejected: "I am suggesting, then, that a kind of latent or hidden naturalism, indeed anthropomorphism, lies at the core of literalist theory [Minimalist theory] and practice. The concept of presence all but says as much. . ." (Fried, p. 19). This is tantamount to an archbishop accusing heretics of having never foresaken the rules of the Church.

What is interesting, particularly in the light of previous attacks by critics on Kinetic Art, is the art establishment's inability to incorporate or even tolerate a sustained time dimension. Origins of this reflect the structure of myth itself. History-oriented myths only exist as points in time, never as sustained events. The success of art history depends upon the reducibility of every work of art, every style, to a finite point or segment in time. As George Kubler observes, works of art do not exist in time, they have an "entry point."

Every paradigm of descriptive analysis eventually eliminates itself as a useful myth because of its failure to mediate past and future, and to provide some intellectually consistent notion of all art. In fact, the lack of coherence within art theories allows the artist some sense of control over the situation, perhaps supplying art with its enigmatic consistency. Synchronic myths are normally cyclical and predictable. But the historical myth of art depends upon its unpredictability. Consequently one of the most useful features of formal descriptive analysis is its inability to connect and analyze seemingly isolated art objects. This is a situation which mutually benefits both historians and artists.

So for the past fifty years—or at least superficially—a certain rapport has existed between artists and art historians, just as long as both enjoyed a mutually beneficial strategy. Not surprisingly, the growing skill with which historians verify and analyze documents, including works of art, prejudices their comprehension of the activities involved. As scholarly books and catalogues seem more thorough and authoritative, their literary and positivistic techniques become pyrotechnical epiphanies to the works under examination. This began naturally enough when nineteenth-century philological techniques were first applied to art records and supporting documents. By the middle of the century, such results were used as materials for general histories of art, and most importantly they served as a methodological basis for the *catalogue raisonné*. Iconographic and formal analyses were thought to be correctives to the documentary emphasis, and subsequently provided invaluable "readings" for individual works of art. However it is increasingly apparent that Formalism consists of early-twentieth-century Behaviorism and Gestalt theory, fused to postclassical but neo-idealist esthetics, and applied to art as a scholarly tool. In the broadest sense there is a direct reciprocity between ideation supporting art and the methods used to analyze it.

Within the last five to ten years some art historians have begun to support an "against interpretation" doctrine through which works of art and perhaps the lives of their originators are studied as sacrosanct texts. Their reasoning is that any attempt to force works of art into a system simply falsifies the artists' intentions and the integrity of their work. On the surface this appears to have merit, except that it amounts to a holding action. In recognizing that the organismic concept of art history is no longer valid, it simply attempts to block any analysis of why it fails. Inherently a conservative theory of art, in the Hegelian sense, it expects a constant evolution of new and significant art images logically connected to the past. Certainly this is a very linear view of Hegel's dialectic which, in fact, anticipated not the mildly and pleasingly unexpected but the radically unexpected. The art historian Arnold Hauser has had much to say about exponents of "art for art's sake" who view art as a closed system, one which would be subject to destruction if it were expanded into the sociological or economic domains. But Hauser misses the essential issue, not that sociopolitical analysis deprives art of its spirituality, but rather that the more the history of art is connected to other areas of human development the more unsatisfactory it becomes as a mythic creation. To remain efficacious myths have to preserve their linearity and crystallinity, adhering to a structural form which can be introduced repeatedly through varying themes.

It appears that Brian O'Doherty was one of the first critics to seriously question the present rupture between art and art history. He speaks of the peculiar situation in which, after having invented art history, we are, as Cioran says, eaten up by it: "The attack on the delusions of historical systems . . . seems to spatialize history, turning it into a landscape or surface containing all events past and present. On this chaotic surface we can inscribe according to our dispositions. History has disappeared in favor of particular forms of chaos" (from a panel discussion presented at the University of Iowa, May 10, 1969). O'Doherty then proceeds to outline the teleological possibilities confronting the art world.

> I. Dialectical history and the post-modernism of (particularly) color-field painting.
> II. Object and Conceptual art, and the anti-historical landscape, [also Process Art] on which order is circumscribed with various modalities of chaos, and vice versa.
> III. Art generally identified with the future, roughly grouping kinetic and technological art, in which the technological imperative and social ideas are frequently cited.

What is noteworthy about O'Doherty's catalogue of possibilities is not its number of styles, since such a plurality has been with us since the end of the last century, but rather that each of these groupings implies an incompatible future with the others.

Style remains the *bête noire* of art history. Rarely do historians concur on the peak decade of the Renaissance, or on the precise transitional dates from Neoclassicism to Romanticism. A theory is still offered to the effect that upheavals of the twentieth century are more or less extensions of the Romantic era. Also a few historians are inclined to view the Bauhaus and C.I.A.M.–influenced architecture of the 1920's as a modernist version of Classicism. As reasonable or misguided as these proposals are, they indicate the historian's urge to categorize events recognizably, and even more, to make those categories consistent and contiguous.

Recently the philosopher and esthetician Morris Weitz investigated the inconsistencies of style as related to Mannerism (Weitz, May, 1970). He shows that out of four authorities cited, no two agree on the antecedents, dates, artists, traits, or significance of Mannerism. Weitz explains that the connotations of *maniera* picked up negative qualities which the term Mannerism still retains. It is almost as though artistic periods are more favorably thought of if they provide distinct chronological visibility and contrasts with surrounding periods. The abstract of Weitz's paper reads: "An examination of the range of disagreement among the historians of Mannerism, especially of the reasons they give for individual works or artists being or not being manneristic, reveals the irreducible vagueness of style concepts that has been overlooked by all art historians who state what style is without comprehending how style-giving reasons actually function in art history" (Weitz, May, 1970). And so the inadequacies of style are sorely felt, as attested by Meyer Schapiro's famous essay on the subject nearly two decades ago (Schapiro, 1953). "How style-giving reasons actually function in art history" remains an unanswered and intriguing question.

In some areas the question has already been met by the refutation of history itself as a social philosophy; this is particularly the case where there is a full awareness of the implications of the Saussurian terms *diachronic* and *synchronic*. According to Lévi-Strauss primitive societies desperately resist changes in their way of life. Alterations occurring stem from either unforeseen environmental conditions or invading "civilizing" forces possessing more sophisticated technology. Most nonliterate societies prefer to live modestly in ecological balance with their environments. These are, in Lévi-Strauss's words, "cold societies," societies which precipitate no perceivable change over time and have no need of a written history; hence they are ahistorical or synchronic in structure. In contrast, a number of "hot societies" have arisen since the Neolithic revolution. Their dynamicism must be attributed to exploration, constant internecine wars, class struggle, and a self-image as evolving flourishing organisms; in a word these are diachronic structures, societies with a sense of history.

Lévi-Strauss proposes that all societies incorporate myths into their customs and information systems, since myths are stabilizing elements in the form of narratives that remain true no matter how many ways they are told. For Lévi-Strauss at least, it is questionable that a diachronic culture can sustain myth, since the longevity of myths depends upon social structures where events are repetitive and unchanging, thus psychically and intellectually the same. History-oriented societies appear to lack the foundation for a stable mythic structure. However Lévi-Strauss is quite aware that myths do exist in literate societies, and suggests that we have just begun to detect the mechanisms by which they operate.

One mechanism by which myths operate in art history is the "genre concept," or the means of classification which isolate artistic events into groups and sub-groups for ease of handling. Style as such acts as a kind of fulcrum between the art object and art history. It mediates the monolithic concept of art history through an infinite number of events and objects which comprise the historical ideal. As shown in Chart I, every diachronic time sequence is "bracketed" by concepts of synchronic time. Diachronic time presupposes that an infinite number of events overlap and fuse with one another in such a way that no physical or self-apparent distinctions are possible. As a result, history-oriented cultures support mythic structures by providing fluid time slots between the monolithic sequences of synchronic time. Newly discovered art objects are, if possible, incorporated into the concepts of object, style and history. When a radical

I. HISTORICAL-MYTHIC STRUCTURES IN ART THROUGH DIACHRONIC-SYNCHRONIC SYNTHESIS

SYNCHRONIC TIME	DIACHRONIC TIME	SYNCHRONIC TIME	DIACHRONIC TIME	SYNCHRONIC TIME
art history	series of styles	style	series of art objects	art object
history	series of eras	historical era	series of events in archives	event

adjustment is necessary, it is made by defining a new stylistic concept, leaving other styles essentially undisturbed. In a similar way older works are adjusted and reevaluated.

Fundamental to the mythic form of art history is the practice whereby all objects are regarded as completely unique. Works of art may neither be divided nor multiplied, although they may relate to other works serially or cyclically. This is true of styles which become linear segments in the span of historical time. In theory it is impossible for objects to occupy the same space in time or place. In a like sense, styles ideally function in sequential fashion. Modern art represents something of a contradiction. Since Impressionism, the plurality of styles has increased to where perhaps a half dozen styles are practiced and accepted concurrently in the art world.

Chronological homogeneity is equally necessary for sustaining the art historical myth. There cannot be more than one art history, since a second would produce conflicting mythic structures. Thus all objects which possess at least some of the traits of art become art objects. Since the turn of the century numerous archeological and anthropological discoveries have inspired an unwieldy situation of a history of global art instead of simply Western art. Hence questions are provoked as to what constitutes art: original esthetic intention or subsequent recognition of esthetic merit? As a result, aboriginal artifacts from Africa, the Western Hemisphere, Asia, and Oceania have at times been closely compared to examples of modernist art. Neither usage nor morphology binds these disparate artifacts together; what does, of course, is that they originate as elements of one mythic form or another and are unconsciously recognized as such. (In this respect it is interesting to speculate on the reasons why children's art is never afforded a place in the "history of art"—particularly since children's art shows affinities with modern art equal to those displayed by so-called primitive and aboriginal art. From a mythic standpoint the reason is that children are incapable of producing art because they do not generate offspring; also their art produces no sense of historical "evolution" but is the result of stages of physical growth.)

All myths include time inversions as necessary features. For example, Plato in his *Phaedo* had a clear conception of immortality. He also developed a dialectic between the single and the continuous (not unlike synchronic and diachronic), both in respect to time and self. Plato believed that essences exist continuously, while elements of human culture strive to become universal ideal forms. Unities exist in continuous time, particulars in sets at given moments.

Plato argued that the human body is composed of parts and activities existing in discrete states temporally. However the soul exists within the body, driving the body as one would drive a car. Since the body is constantly in a state of becoming, it must be a discrete form evolving through time, while the soul is a continuous unique form. With death the body disintegrates. But because the soul exists essentially, it cannot be decomposed and so it lives on. Christian eschatology is consequently the perfect narrative to legitimize Plato's theory of immortality.

In *The Will to Power,* Friedrich Nietzsche develops an argument contradictory to the basis of Christian logic (Nietzsche, p. 549). He disproves the existence of God by attacking the concept that every moment is discrete and singular. Nietzsche argues that matter is finite in the universe, but that time is infinite. Because a given number of parts can be combined only in a finite number of ways—while producing a large number—every possible combination of those parts would occur (assuming a state of equilibrium is never reached, which obviously has not happened because the world is still changing and has already evolved from no known point in time). As a result, every combination would be tried for an infinite duration of time. Permutations of a particular sequence are generated according to the power of the number of events and configurations involved. Still this results in a finite number. Therefore every possible sequence would by necessity be repeated over an infinite period of time. (It follows from Nietzsche's argument that the same person is destined to live the same life an infinite number of times!)

We may quarrel with Nietzsche's physics and cosmology, and with good reason, but he remains one of the first philosophers attempting to undermine the logic behind mythic structures. Using Plato's assumptions, Nietzsche destroys the concept of a continuous and essential soul by maintaining a contrary concept, the idea that each event in a person's life is a unique and discrete combination of circumstances. Plato's soul could never repeat its activities through other bodies. Nietzsche removes the possibility of spiritual control over unlimited time and replaces it with his Superman, that single individual whose will-to-power places him, for the moment, in control of the destinies of others. As a mythic form, and one identical with the technological demiurge, Nietzsche shifts meaning from eternal life to absolute power over the present.

This same reciprocity is inherent in the relationships between artist and art historian. The reward of an art activity is instant control over the moment by the individual, via the mediating agency of art history. Successful artistic creation in the historical sense invalidates every preceding creation by making it obsolete. Parallel to this Christianity uses the destruction of one life in order to sustain many existences eternally. Art performs a similar inversion. It becomes the product of a single man instead of whole societies, so that art objects give pleasure to all men at all times. The legitimacy of the artist depends upon his discovering the right approach to using signs in order to make objects (Kubler's "positional value") at a given time in history. Out of this emerges a mythic trade-off between artist and art historian. Each important artist is given control over segments of time in the continuum of art history, and in exchange the historian gains control over ideal time, past and future. The meaning is obvious. As Lévi-Strauss suggests, mythologies establish constraints over an eternal present. Yet he resists saying that history-oriented mythologies presume to regulate the past, and thereby to some extent the future. As time goes by artists intuitively begin to formulate rules according to the historical myth, filling in necessary terms of the logic-structure. Art history, like the soul in Plato's *Phaedo,* demands treatment as a continuous and evolving ideal. The notion of a perpetual ideal corresponds with the avant-garde artist's expression of the essential cohesiveness of elements in his art. Equally mythic is the Nietzschean position that ideal expression takes the form of finite, repeated assertions of power in a particular time and place.

So apparently all attempts to categorize events produce tendencies toward a mythic structure. Nevertheless this remains an unresolved issue since the very nature of such categories presumes that a "language" or a point of view is inevitable. George Kubler in *The Shape of Time* displays more awareness of this predicament than many of his colleagues. With considerable objectivity he discusses the weaknesses of most historical techniques. His own particular bias possibly stems from a fondness for art historian Henri Focillon. He would, if possible, translate Focillon's organic metaphor into a set of scientific techniques for examining the formal properties of all kinds of artifacts, not just works of art. As an archaeologist Kubler senses the synthetic character of the distinctions which make some objects works of art and others not. (It is in fact this very arbitrariness which subtracts credibility from the art historical concept.) Kubler's morphological scheme is based upon the inventive uniqueness of objects in a series. And it is in this mathematical comprehension of the series that Kubler uncovers one of the major fallacies of creativity. He notes that from the "inside" (that is, within the context of art history) most classes appear to be open sequences, therefore infinite; while from the "outside" they seem to be closed series. The implication is that modern art is a semiblind endeavor moving as a series toward zero or infinity. In any case its terms limit all succeeding terms in the same historical series. Kubler in another context cites the rules of series: "(1) in the course of an irreversible finite series the use of any position reduces the number of remaining positions; (2) each position in a series affords only a limited number of possibilities of action; (3) the choice of an action commits the corresponding position; (4) taking a position both defines and reduces the range of possibilities in the succeeding position" (Kubler, p. 54). Periodology, according to one authority, Kubler (p. 105), is a totally arbitrary convenience determined mainly by esthetic considerations.

Kubler ends his book by reflecting that "style is like a rainbow. It is a phenomenon of perception governed by the coincidence of certain physical conditions. We can see it only briefly while we pause between sun and the rain, and it vanishes when we go to the place where we thought we saw it. Whenever we think we grasp it, as in the work of an individual painter, it dissolves into the further perspectives of the work of that painter's predecessors or his followers. . ." (p. 129). Like all myths, the concepts of style and art history possess vitality and heroism as long as they remain *lived* ideas; once opened to close examination in the face of contradictions, they dissolve before our eyes.

A STRUCTURAL APPROACH TO ART

If the essence of science, ethics, language, and ceremony is conceptual relationships, then the same might be true of art. Approached on this level, we must accept the possibility that art operates according to an unperceived and unconventional scheme of logic. If finding it seems formidable, this is because the fusion of visual forms makes it difficult to separate themes, plastic elements, and levels of reasoning into tractable categories.

Yet if the syntagm-system relationships of iconic works are definable, then the task of locating structure is not insurmountable. In fact, the supporting logic reveals itself with increasing clarity as we examine contemporary art, which has discarded most of the traditional signifying terms.

Until recently art remained a source of social cohesion, as is totemism, gift-giving, and the exchange of women between clans. So in spite of all that appears disruptive about modernism, art represents stable communication within a society. Therefore the avant-garde and its demise is more than a failing institution; it signifies perhaps the inability of a particular mythic form to endure any longer, and perhaps all mythic forms connected to it.

For verification consider the place of art in postclassical times. In the centuries just after the first millennium A.D., the function of two- and three-dimensional imagery was patently totemic. Art served the Church; its didactic goal was to inspire and instruct the faithful in doctrines of the day, merging both spiritual and secular law through biblical narrative. Examples of Byzantine and medieval art permit us to understand the meaning of the term *icon:* in its most literal sense, the portrayal of sacred imagery which invests objects with the magical potency of the ideas represented. In icons, illustrated books, stained glass, mosaics, and other religious artifacts, the conceptual power of a theme determined a viewer's capacity to identify sacred properties with objects themselves.

If anything, the vaunted perfection of classical ideals during the Renaissance represents a diminution of religious rapport through the medium of objects. Consequently pictorial innovations of relative size, vanishing points, spatial depth, natural coloration, shadows, and aerial perspective were most apt for an age with less conviction in the myths and dogmas portrayed. Representation of religious ideals and their earthly counterparts gave way to thinly disguised depictions of the real world. There is significance in the fact that through the seventeenth, eighteenth, and nineteenth centuries—that is, during the decline of religious expression—the academies promoted historical and mythological themes as the noblest and most important subject matter available to the artist. The depictions of genre themes, still-lifes, living individuals, and landscapes were second-rate enterprises. Thus in a matter of four centuries (the thirteenth to the seventeenth century), Western art evolved from the unemotional stereotypes and psychological neutrality of complete religious conviction to portrayal of vivid, intimate scenes of everyday life, with the academic tradition of overt mythology as a bridge between the two. The significance of the academic tradition is this: mythical fables and historical incidents refer to events which are obviously mythic and hence proper materials for art. Not until the nineteenth century, though, was there general recognition that the activities of great artists could in themselves comprise the substance of myth. Yet this in effect was what various artists had implied through their work from Rembrandt onward.

A case has been made for the deterioration of realistic painting following the invention of the daguerreotype in 1839. But it would seem that the decline of Renaissance conventions had already begun at least two centuries before in Dutch painting. What the photograph did, as Delacroix attested, was to offer painters an infallable imitation of reality which they could never hope to duplicate. Thus the result was frustration and, in some quarters, fierce opposition to photography. So that the optical-chemical duplication of actual events simply encouraged a tendency away from realism which had been at work in artist's minds for centuries. Some academicians attempted to match the photograph's infinite graduations of values and detail. Yet ironically painters like Manet, Degas, and Cézanne perceived the full meaning of the camera in its ability to flatten spaces, eliminate shadows, and catch moving forms slightly off balance.

From at least the sixteenth century the *camera obscura* (a box through which a pinpoint opening projected an actual image onto a screen) was used by artists. Thus draftsmen had the means of verifying pictorial compositions with faithful images of their models. In fact it seems reasonable that only a culture impelled to imitate the results of a camera would have bothered to develop this particular piece of technology. So acculturated are we to photographic realism that anthropologists and psychologists have realized only recently that pictorial illusionism depends upon visual cues just as innately abstract as examples of primitive or modernist art (Segall, Campbell, and Herskovits, 1966, pp. 3–22, 209–14). Nevertheless psychologists of esthetics such as Rudolf Arnheim have consistently attempted formalist or atomistic approaches to visual reconstruction. In *Art and Visual Perception* (1954) Arnheim decomposes pictorial vision into balance, shape, form, growth, space, light, color, movement, tension and expression. Here he explains the mechanics of abstraction by examining the properties of visual elements one by one. Abstraction in such cases (Arnheim, 1969, pp. 51–53) is nearly always described in terms of optical deviation from the norm, that is, including types of distortion. Of course this presumes, from a formalist point of view, that all depictions of reality are abstract except reality itself. Moreover, this theory only accounts for some of the more local distortions found in avant-garde painting and sculpture during the first decades of the present century. How does it explain the fact that many modern artists feel that *their work recomposes reality in its quintessential form,* rather than deviates from reality?

Consequently perceptualist explanations, even the most scientific, never reveal the origins of artistic transformation which we call "abstraction." Again, relying upon Lévi-Strauss's terms, artists paint pictures not because they are "good to see" but rather because they are "good to think." Works of art are totems which systematically define themselves by their associations with other works. These relationships are perceptual habits which enable us to embody some aspect of outer reality in the objects seen. Thus mechanical and aerial perspective, local color, shape relationships, figure-ground construction, body-object associations, and the making and conceptualization of art are all incorporated into the totemic structure. What we think of as "Modern Art" is simply the tradition of discarding these conventions one by one. Art is a system which allows for the assimilation or rejection of any kind of content, providing the encoding is accomplished through the rules of historical innovation.

As stated earlier, the method by which relationships between signifiers and signifieds are shifted or dropped is Barthes's "transgression." Repeating his definition, transgressions are "the extension of a paradigm on to the syntagmatic plane. . . ." Quite broadly this means that artists uniquely systematize certain relationships within a work of art, while dropping or neutralizing other systems. The substrata for all formal relationships are the mimetic conventions listed above; all avant-garde art attempts to depart from the mean of realistic duplication, that is, photographic illusionism. It becomes obvious that the goal of personal expression pervading postclassical art is an ever-greater degree of departure from exact imitation. Hence historical pressure eventually forces most artists to attempt to disrupt the heterogeneity of the syntagmatic plane, thus altering the normal "speech patterns" of art.

In later stages of modernist art "transgression" has another meaning. This is a reversal of Barthes's definition. Some circumstances occur in which the syntagmatic plane completely dominates systemic or cultural decisions. The concept of the ready-made is a prime example. In this instance the artist systematizes nothing, instead the consistency of the chosen object determines the paradigmatic plane in its entirety.

In art there are two types of transgression: we will classify these as *formal transgression* and *historical transgression*. So far mention has been made only of the first. In the modernist idiom this serves as the backbone of Formalism. Thus subject matter, but more importantly composition, figure-ground relationships, color, scale, and tactile values are all accepted means of transgressing whatever happens to be considered normal art. Most of the great innovators of the nineteenth and twentieth centuries—Manet, Courbet, Monet, Van Gogh, Cézanne, Rodin, Picasso, Matisse, Mondrian, and Pollock—have committed important formal transgressions. By comparison, historical transgressions are mainly misunderstood, or more accurately, not comprehended at all. There is an interesting reason for this. Formal transgressions are based on literary and plastic innovations which perpetuate the illusion of historical change; historical transgressions are essentially structural disruptions subverting the temporal myth of art; that is, they destroy the illusion that art progresses from one stage to the next through time. Historical transgressions, to use Marcel Duchamp's term, "short-circuit" the evolution of formal transgressions. And quite obviously, Duchamp was the first artist to employ historical transgressions as a matter of strategy. Here there are several approaches; the most common is the production of works which are far ahead of their time historically and remain unexplained, that is, the ready-mades again. Art may also transgress various barriers of the art myth, for instance art which is art through its deliberate *non-uniqueness,* or dialectical use of seriality. Another example would be works which focus on the time element but in such a way that time is negated or reduced to a finite duration (it must be remembered that mythically, works of art function only as points on the time continuum, never as events). Artists who use historical transgressions consistently usually have an exceptional intuitive grasp of the structural rules of art. Presently Daniel Buren and Les Levine should be included in this category. However Conceptual Art also has produced several artists engaged in historically transgressive art.

Before 1870 avant-gardism was a matter of individual temperament and idiosyncrasy. Painters such as Delacroix, Turner, Courbet, and Manet were psychologically motivated to create as they did. But with Impressionism the programmatic and collective aspects of extreme formal transgressive behavior began to exert themselves. From the accompanying diagram (II) it is predicated that the exponential take-off point for art historical consciousness is about 1910. The very gradual linear rise and subsequent take-off is, of course, a nonmathematical approximation of how artists have synchronized their thinking with the historical imperative of avant-gardism. It would seem from the analyses appearing in the next chapter that, aside from Duchamp, conscious realization of the historical myth began to appear through Linguistic Conceptualism in 1967 or 1968.

II. RISE OF HISTORICAL CONSCIOUSNESS IN THE MAKING OF ART

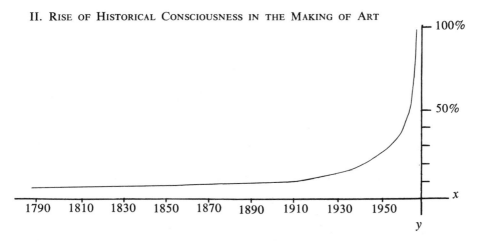

Thus shortly after, art historical consciousness reached 100 percent, or saturation.

In the course of this study it was proposed that Lévi-Strauss's convention of Natural/Cultural opposition represents the fundamental dichotomy mediated by myth. All activities, concepts, and linguistic divisions discussed may be divided into either one or the other. The accompanying chart (III) divides terms as they have been used by Lévi-Strauss and Barthes.

In general these consist of sets of categories standardly applied for the purposes of making linguistical, semiological and anthropological analyses. We have found that slightly different divisions are more applicable to art. Specifically these are concerned with planning, making, perceiving, and situating works of art. To some extent the categories in our chart (IV) tend to overlap. Moreover it seems likely that there are oppositions not included in this chart.

Before making a structural analysis, it must be emphasized that successful art serves the same mediating function as myth. Consequently the simple group transformations used by Lévi-Strauss to decode mythic forms are also applicable to art. By defining a work's signifiers and signifieds in their proper order we perform the first step toward reconciling the opposition between physical reality and the esthetic ideals employed by a work of art.

As Lévi-Strauss insists, religion and magic are inseparable; one cannot survive without the other: "For, although it can, in a sense, be said that religion consists in a *humanization of natural laws* and magic in a *naturalization of human actions*—the treatment of certain human actions *as if* they were an integral part of physical determinism—these are not alternatives or stages in an evolution. The anthropomorphism of nature (of which religion consists) and the physiomorphism of man (by which we have defined magic) constitutes two components which are always given, and vary only in proportion" (Lévi-Strauss, 1962a, p. 221). Art is simply another case of the conjunction of religion and magic, a language expressing the effects of both through its own internal logic. In Lévi-Strauss's definition of magic, the *naturalization of human actions* could be expressed as "naturalization of the cultural"; *humanization of natural laws* is the "culturalization of the natural." It becomes evident in the course of the following analyses that all successful art integrates both effects as equally and fully as possible. The reason for such analyses, therefore, is to determine where and how this is done in each case. Whereas all signs are divided into cultural or natural terms, cultural terms culturalize their natural counterparts and natural terms naturalize the cultural. Where either does not clearly occur, the art may be culturalized or naturalized on the

III. Division of Natural and Cultural Terms as Used by Claude Lévi-Strauss and Roland Barthes

	NATURAL	CULTURAL
	Synchronic time	Diachronic time
	Continuous elements	Discrete elements
	All elements as they are found in nature (a continuum without differentiation)	Classifications of elements into conceptually useful systems (as a series of sets)
LÉVI-STRAUSS:	Female	Male
	That which is a signifier (noise, color, line, spoken words, etc.)	That which is signified (language, specific form, tonality, singing, etc.)
	Signifier	Signified
	Syntagm (contrasts)	Paradigm or System (relationships)
	Speech	Language
	Connotation	Denotation
BARTHES:	Phoneme: lexicological units	Morpheme: grammatical units
	Unmotivated signs	Motivated signs
	Plane of expression	Plane of content
	Work	Reward

IV. Division of Natural and Cultural Terms Applied to Art Analysis

NATURAL	CULTURAL
All "real" physical entities	The decision as concept
Assertion of the artist's activities	Assertion of the viewer's perception
Continuous time	The instant (no time)
Movement within the work (either suggested by the artist's activities or the subject matter)	Fixed positions within the work
Ground	Figure
Emotion	Meaning
Mixed series, contrasts, and random units	The unit, object, and sets of oppositions within a system
Environmental	Antienvironmental
(unperceived whole)	(perceived parts of the whole)

ideological plane, or its structure may remain ambiguous, or it may not function as art at all.

A painting by Joseph Albers is chosen for this introductory analysis because Albers's art depends upon a logic form typical of avant-garde art of the last decade, while also being somewhat more complex. In all of his *Homage to the Square* series, variables are reduced to one: color relationships. The "art" of Albers's painting stems from two criteria. Its compositional simplicity through concentric squares relates it to the field paintings of Barnett Newman, Mark Rothko, and Kenneth Noland. Here the important formal similarity is a lack of asymmetrical, unbalanced forms operating in *both dimensions* of the painting—such as in the compositions of Miró, Klee, or de Kooning. The other important feature of Albers's painting is his use of set relationships. A set is a series of entities with at least one attribute in common. Many contemporary painters and sculptors employ the notion of simple sets or simple arrays of objects or panels. Albers is not unique in making nonobjective art using connected subsets. In other words, within one of the "Homage" series, color can be divided into two groups which in turn are connected by a specific attribute shared by at least one color of each group.

Joseph Albers, Study for Homage to the Square: Closing, *1964. Oil on board, 15 13/16 x 15 13/16". Collection, Solomon R. Guggenheim Museum, New York.*

JOSEPH ALBERS: Study for Homage to the Square: Closing (1964)

NATURAL	CULTURAL
(1A) Albers paints on the rough side of an untempered masonite board primed with six coats of white ground; he uses only a palette knife to apply the paint which comes directly from a tube with rarely any admixture of colors	Using cadmium red scarlet overpainted with cadmium red light, cadmium orange (Newmaster), and cadmium yellow, Albers brackets the two intermediary oranges between the yellow and red center square so that they appear to be the same, making three connected subsets
(1B) Albers paints four horizontally acentric squares on a square masonite board	The bilaterally asymmetrical image employed by Albers fulfills the Gestalt required for a specific stage in nonobjective painting
(2) The material object from the painting series *Homage to the Square*	*The title of this study,* Closing, *is derived from the optical merger created between the two intermediary orange squares in a nearly concentric format*
(3) *Albers's articles and books about his work and theory of color interaction*	Albers's research in color underlines both the conscious and intuitive logic employed in his visual reorganization of the world; Albers is primarily a phenomenological structuralist; he eschews the term "Op artist"

The chart above is an inverted form of the system used by Barthes to distinguish levels of signifiers and signifieds. If duplicated according to Barthes's schematic conventions (see p. 25), it would appear as in Chart V, on the following page.

V. A Metalanguage System as It Applies to Works of Art with a Double "Real System"

(3) *System of* *Rhetoric* (Connotation)	SIGNIFIER: The most authoritative writing about the art work as a categorical description			SIGNIFIED: The esthetic ideology behind the art work in terms of style, school, and philosophy
(2) *System of* *Articulation* (Denotation)	SIGNIFIER: The art object signifying the experience	SIGNIFIED: The "content" of the art work through the experience received		
(1) *The Real* *System B*		SIGNIFIER: Content	SIGNIFIED: Artist's intention	*Plane of* *Content*
		Making process	Logical relation	*Plane of* *Expression*
The Real *System A*		Content	Artist's intention	*Plane of* *Content*
		Making process	Logical relation	*Plane of* *Expression*

Throughout the next chapter the modified chart will be used, although sometimes only the first system will be included in schematic form. In all instances where words in a column are italicized, this means that a particular set of terms absorbs the content of the system or systems above it, thus defining a connotative or metalanguage system as it would appear in staggered form. In some cases, particularly with art works of the nineteenth century, higher level systems are added to works which have recognizable content and thus adequate signifieds. These works are structurally complete on the plane of the Real System, but since they are to some degree "abstracted" from pictorial realism, they also contain latent ideological implications. This serves as a bridge between early-nineteenth-century art and completely nonobjective art of the next century. It should be mentioned that in the progress of *Système de la mode* Barthes shortly drops the convention of diagramming the fashion system. In fact, it is probably only defined as a kind of notational convenience for other forays into structural relationships. In the following chapter, however, we will use the diagram form for two reasons. First, our analysis of art is both horizontal and vertical, including many styles and approaches *in time*. Second, it seems important to decompose signifiers and signifieds (natural and cultural elements) in various artists' work, because in many instances these are by no means superficially evident.

In returning to the semiotic diagram of *Study for Homage to the Square: Closing,* several features are noteworthy. In both Real Systems (A and B) the Plane of Content is missing. In all cases where a plane is missing, a horizontal line will be drawn to indicate the omission. The fact that there are two parts to the Real System reveals that Albers's painting must be considered "art" by two separate criteria. However, the reader must refer back to the signifier and signified in the System of Articulation to find the "content" for the painting. These substitute for the missing Plane of Content. For every form of nonobjective art, the second level metalanguage or denotative signifier is *always* the art object itself. Any single level Real System can only refer to itself (in a specific art context) and *not* to subject matter outside itself. Subject matter for nonobjective art can only be introduced through language (a metalanguage form).

It can be stated axiomatically that when only the Plane of Expression is present in a work, the artist has *naturalized the cultural,* that is *expressed* some perceptual relationships without alluding to content (i.e., *culturalizing the natural*). Hand-facturing or primitiveness are not always necessary elements of naturalization. The process of bringing an idea into material existence *is naturalization*. The validity of nonobjective art depends upon structural relations found in color, form, and composition. Articulation of these relations depends upon varying degrees of freedom in the making process.

Two crucial types of relations must exist between the signifiers and signifieds of the Real System. First, there must be a direct causal relationship between the signifiers and their signifieds. Second, there must be a firm relation through *analogy* between the signifiers and signifieds of the two planes. In effect, this represents the commutation test for a nonlinguistic semiotic. Where a Metalanguage or Denotative System substitutes for the missing Plane of Content or Plane of Expression, then it takes the place of the missing plane in the structural equation. Thus there is an analogous, but not equal, relation between the Plane of Content and the Plane of Expression.

$$\frac{\text{Signified (CONTENT)}}{\text{Signifier (CONTENT)}} \;\backsimeq\; \frac{\text{Signified (EXPRESSION)}}{\text{Signifier (EXPRESSION)}}$$

Albers's painting requires two equations since there are two parts to the Real System.

EMPIRICAL		ESTHETIC
$\dfrac{\text{The perception of color relations (Denotation)}}{\text{The finished painting as object (Denotation)}}$	$\backsimeq$	$\dfrac{\text{Four colors composed in three connected subsets (Real System A)}}{\text{Fabrication of the painting (Real System A)}}$
$\dfrac{\text{Perception of reduced formal relations (Denotation)}}{\text{The finished painting as object (Denotation)}}$	$\backsimeq$	$\dfrac{\text{Four squares bilaterally arranged on an asymmetrical axis (Real System B)}}{\text{Fabrication of the painting (Real System B)}}$

Above the two equations are the headings *Empirical* and *Esthetic*. Such a convention is used by Lévi-Strauss to define the terms of a myth. The *Empirical* refers to hypotheses and statements that *seem* to have a basis in the real world by virtue of the myth (or art) itself. The *Esthetic*, or *Mythical*, according to Lévi-Strauss, is the logic behind the physical assembly of the myth (or art work). Art's credibility stems from the analogical connection between making and assertion. This relationship implies an interdependence: the *Empirical* always lends a concrete plausibility to the art object by attaching it to circumstances outside of itself, while the *Esthetic* somehow physically duplicates these circumstances, thus adding an air of implausibility or magic to the *Empirical*.

As we shall see at the beginning of the next chapter, Albers's painting represents a particular form of double structure appearing only near the end of the evolution of nonobjective art. Normally where there is a repetition of the Real System in art, it accompanies some form of representational art. One can account for art's avant-garde condition by understanding how artists create new signs by *neutralizing* the content or formal relations found in the signs of previous art. The type of structural analysis used in this study cannot reveal the underlying mechanisms of perception that account for significant changes in art. This will be a subject of a future book. The analyses in the present book are basically synchronic. However, by sensing the shifting esthetic and material requirements of artists, the reader can begin to grasp the general tendencies underlying reductivist esthetics. The limited number of works chosen for this study is by no means exhaustive. If anything, it represents a cross-section of art considered significant by the art-conscious sector of the American public.

Let us summarize briefly what has been said so far: the mythic structure of art is reconstituted through a binary system of *Natural* and *Cultural* attributes, which describe the Real System. Every work of art depends upon two or more signs with analogical relations between them. All figurative works of art have a reciprocity between motivated and unmotivated signs. No art is more or less "advanced"; rather, art which seems to be the most progressive at a given time has simply discarded the greatest number of signifying conventions. Art appears historical for two reasons: first, because of its frequent connection to notions of progress, technical sophistication, and contemporaneousness; second, because of its broad connection to human psychology where viewers unconsciously anticipate the negation of signifying conventions in "new" art.

As in totemism, the purpose of art is to separate man from the undifferentiated consistency of Nature, bringing a certain order to the environment as it is conceived. Through the unifying force of analogy, art provides a medium through which man defines the same kinds of divisions that occur in the formation of language, kinship, trade relationships, myth, and other essentially cultural systems. Art is symbolic play of the highest order of importance. It gives each culture a barometer of sorts, indicating the health and stability of its civilizing customs and structures.

III

Structural Analyses

Structuralism is the search for unsuspected harmonies. It is the discovery of a system of relations latent in a series of objects.

—HAYES AND HAYES
Claude Lévi-Strauss (p. 4)

THE STRUCTURAL MATRIX

So far it has been hypothesized that all art is based on a quaternary structure where two terms are analogously equal to two other terms. The example of the Albers painting in the previous chapter implies that there are a number of variations within this four-part structure. We might call this the matrix of logic modes controlling the making of art. Twenty years ago the Bourbaki mathematicians developed a group of theorems pertaining to the algebra of sets. Independently, Lévi-Strauss has used some of the same ideas for defining kinship relations and mythic forms. These Klein Group concepts have subsequently been used by other semiologists. The universality of Klein Group mathematics leads one to suspect that the human brain possesses an innate faculty for partitioning meaningful relations into groups of four. But this is far from proven.

We hypothesize that the most basic logic of a work of art follows the form of the proposition: *the sign of the Plane of Content (signified/signifier) is analogously equivalent to the sign of the Plane of Expression (signified/signifier).* This is written so that Content *(C)* $\backsim$ Expression *(E)*.

Klein Groups are four-part structures: an identity transformation plus three permutative transformations. The consistency of such a structure is always the result of permutations derived from one or two operations on a single function. For example, x may be changed to $-x$ (one operation), and its inverse $1/x$ (the second operation), while the only permutation of the two operations is $-1/x$. It has been proposed that the simplest function is $C = E$. But suppose that the most basic function is $n(C) = n'(E)$, or one or more *Planes of Content* are equivalent to one or more *Planes of Expression*. (Briefly, this implies that the preferred cultural mode in sentence structure or works of art consists of multiple propositions, or propositions which have more than a single idea.) Below we have formulated a Klein Group based on the identity $n(C) = n'(E)$. (See "On the Meaning of the Word Structure in Mathematics," by Marc Barbut, in *Structuralism,* Basic Books, New York, 1970, pp. 367–388.)

Given the semiotic equation $n(C) = n'(E)$, there is its opposite $n(C) \neq n'(E)$; there is also the omission of coefficients, $C = E$, and finally the product of these two operations, $C \neq E$. In the following analyses we have substituted the alchemical agents for the equations and the structures they represent. There is reasonable evidence for this alignment in alchemical literature.

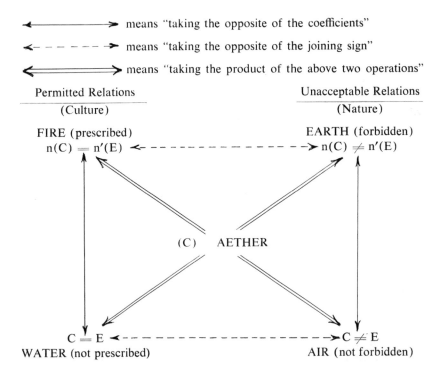

means "taking the opposite of the coefficients"

means "taking the opposite of the joining sign"

means "taking the product of the above two operations"

Permitted Relations	Unacceptable Relations
(Culture)	(Nature)

FIRE (prescribed)   EARTH (forbidden)

$n(C) = n'(E)$ $n(C) \neq n'(E)$

(C)   AETHER

$C = E$ $C \neq E$

WATER (not prescribed)   AIR (not forbidden)

In semiotic logic there are certain *implied* relations between the functions defined by the solid-line arrows. WATER implies FIRE, but not the reverse. Similarly, AIR implies EARTH, but not the reverse. The five elements define the five types of equations controlling language form having two planes. These elements are mutually exclusive except under certain conditions not revealed by their algebraic forms. For instance, the Albers painting is a conjunction of AIR and EARTH thereby giving the illusion of FIRE. Disjunctive relations consist of two types: the disjunction of *contraries,* indicated by the dotted-line arrows (equations with a single difference between them), and the disjunction of *contradictories,* indicated by the double-line arrows (equations with two differences between them). The other possible conjunction lies between FIRE and EARTH where the surface meaning of an artwork has a second esoteric meaning, usually defined by hermetic symbolism or a hidden set of relations.

The multiple structure of FIRE, $n(C) = n'(E)$, provides us with the following four-part relationships:

SIGNIFIERS	SIGNIFIEDS		
Content	Artist's Intention	CONTENT	
Making Process	Logical Relation	EXPRESSION	*FIRST KERNEL*

Content	Artist's Intention	CONTENT	
Making Process	Logical Relation	EXPRESSION	*SECOND KERNEL*

In contrast WATER, $C = E$, refers to two-plane semiotic systems using only a single kernel structure. The element AIR, $C \neq E$, refers to all semiotic structures possessing a Plane of Expression but no Plane of Content. Within various semiotic systems AIR appears to have a Plane of Content. However, this takes the form of a *metalanguage* or Denotative Plane. All nonobjective art depends upon a metalanguage support in the form of the artist's or critic's elaborations as to its meaning or intrinsic content. In all instances $C \neq E$ means that the "Plane of Content" (Metalanguage) is not analogous or equivalent to the Plane of Expression.

Description of Object	Metalanguage Description		
			CONTENT
	Making Process	Neutralizing Function	EXPRESSION

The most obscure and least preferred semiotic equation belongs to EARTH, $n(C) \neq n'(E)$. With EARTH the making process is not at all important; the consistency of relationships between various items of the work's content is important. Hence, the Plane of Content is divorced from the Plane of Expression. Such art functions without the usual planes because its logic depends upon the viewer perceiving at least *two sets,* each containing a minimum of three members. Thus what is important with EARTH is the interrelations between entities or attributes of entities defining the substance or content of the art. If *a, b,* and *c* are subset members of a set, then these relations within the Venn diagram below assume the following algebraic form:

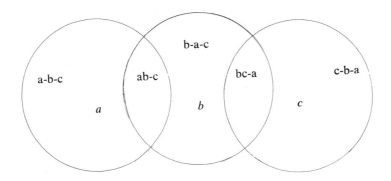

The fifth element AETHER, *(C),* has a special significance since it possesses a Plane of Content, but lacks a Plane of Expression. It was the genius of Marcel Duchamp which deduced this element and incorporated it into works of art in the form of the ready-made. He contracted the term from de Saussure's expression for ritualistic or contexturally complete phrases, *"locutions toutes faites."* Thus the ready-made is always a manufactured object with both natural-cultural *and* sacred-profane connotations. The structure of AETHER *(C)* is as follows:

Ritual Integration of Everyday Activities		Equilibration of the Four Principles	CONNOTATION
Content	Artist's Intention		CONTENT
			EXPRESSION

In all the ancient philosophies of Western hermeticism AETHER remains the preferred semiotic structure because its selection implies that the person choosing it has a knowledge of the entire Klein Group matrix and its social implications. AETHER signifies perfect balance and self-knowledge.

Within the span of styles making up modernist art various ideas demand different elements. For instance, we find FIRE apparent in some Surrealism, Dadaism, hermetic and religious art; WATER appears in much of the figurative avant-garde art of the nineteenth and twentieth centuries; AIR represents all the schools of nonobjective art, including Suprematism, Constructivism, *de Stijl,* Abstract Expressionism, Color-Field painting, Object Art, and Process Art. EARTH frequently defines the art of Surrealism, Dadaism, and recently much Conceptual and Ecological Art.

The reader must remember that the analyses to follow are essentially synchronic; thus they reveal no direct causality between works. As we have mentioned previously, diachronic shifts between succeeding styles demand a more comprehensive study. These analyses support two basic tenets of the social sciences: firstly, any social system that operates according to consensus and tacit acceptance of qualitative criteria may be defined by laws, although such laws may be in effect unconsciously; secondly, if we can show that a fairly large sampling of art works conforms to the Klein Group matrix, then we have reasonable evidence that the human mind operates in part according to corresponding patterns of logic. These analyses are not conclusive; they are a beginning.

For Lévi-Strauss the most fundamental binary opposition continues to be the "Cultural" (FIRE and WATER) and the "Natural" (AIR and EARTH). Within the hermetic tradition these are referred to as "Cosmos" (Culture) and "Chaos" (Nature). We have used these in place of *Signifier* and *Signified* in the analyses. It must be reemphasized that the above terms correspond to a very broad set of dichotomies defining on one hand *pure perception,* and on the other, *perception modified by intelligent thought.*

1. J. M. W. TURNER: Rain, Steam and Speed—Great Western Railroad (1844)

NATURAL	CULTURAL
The atmospheric effects of a coal-burning train passing over a bridge in the rain	Turner probably got the idea for this painting while traveling on the Exeter-London railroad, at a time when the train was passing through Maidenhead during a rainstorm
Turner painted by gradually building up vortices of natural elements around a cultural theme; quite often the theme was no more than an excuse for the presentation of fantastic atmospheric effects; these are usually achieved with impastos of white paint (representing pure light to the artist) scumbled over or glazed with powdered pigments; the consistency of the paint is usually granular and washy rather than fluid	As well as any of the artist's later works, *Rain, Steam and Speed* defines the constant confrontation between man and nature; time and the flux of conditions are reflected in Turner's rejection of realistic naturalism and in this instance by the peculiar fading perspective of the train rushing across the bridge; Turner uses cultural elements such as ships, buildings, or human figures because they alone define the effects of nature by standing in opposition to them

1. J. M. W. Turner, Rain, Steam and Speed—Great Western Railroad, *1844. Oil on canvas, 35¾ x 48". Collection, The National Gallery, London.*

In the case of Turner's *Rain, Steam and Speed* it is evident that the Natural-Cultural mediation is internalized in terms of content (Turner drew back from pure landscapes or seascapes), and externalized through procedure. The idea of making a painting of a train passing over a bridge is a culturalization of the natural; but Turner naturalizes his subject matter in an altogether modern fashion. With much contemporary painting *the act of painting* becomes the means of naturalization. This is certainly true of Turner's later canvases where the painting activity is expressly made into a sign. It is known that by 1835 Turner would often "finish" his paintings at the annual academy exhibitions on varnishing days. Usually these days were used to add the last coats of varnish before the opening date. But with little more than a faintly washed sketch on his canvas, Turner would create one of his atmospheric seascapes before a crowd of spectators there, adding historical or mythological subject matter as needed. Plainly he wanted people to see that these interpretations of nature's visual effects were creations of his mind and hand. *Rain, Steam and Speed* in his words, "set a man-made construction in the midst of the warring elements of nature."

Historically Turner's thinking was out of context by at least thirty years. But by 1877 the Impressionists could well appreciate his vision as masterly (in a letter addressed to Sir Coutts Lindsay after he had founded the Grosvenor Gallery in London). What Turner did intuitively, later artists would do purposefully. Increasingly, modern artists have created sign systems of stronger and stronger oppositions. Significantly enough, the excuse for this has always been to effect greater realism and less illusionism.

If we reduce the terms of the Natural-Cultural structure of Turner's painting to their simplest form, the following over/under structural relationships become apparent:

EMPIRICAL		ESTHETIC
Artist's impressions of the contrasting turbulance of the weather and modern transportation	≎	The juxtaposition of Nature and Culture
Fusion of Natural and Cultural atmospheric effects		Atmospheric effects simulated through painting technique

2. EDOUARD MANET: MLLE. VICTORINE IN THE COSTUME OF AN ESPADA (1862)

NATURAL	CULTURAL
A young woman dressed as an espada in a bull ring	Manet decides to paint a full-length portrait of a young woman dressed as an espada; the situation makes it evident that she is posing as a model, thus subtracting any historical or anecdotal pretensions from the painting; however, the composition is established through a close examination of several prints in Goya's Tauromaquin series, following the popularity of the day for Spanish themes
With a few striking exceptions, the painting is generally somber; the figure is a study of black and white contrasts with touches of pastel color, while background consists of black, dull grays, and browns; vividness and direct brushwork give this painting an immediacy which most artists of the period would consider vulgar or inartistic; Manet uses neither underpainting nor finishing varnish, so that the paint represents paint itself; he undermines naturalism by using flat uncolored tones, large areas of local color, and violent tonal and value contrasts; because of a general absence of modeling, the painting would appear in its day to be somewhat incredible	Manet liked Japanese composition and had little sympathy for mechanical perspective, which perhaps explains why the horse and picador in mid-ground are too small for the scale of the rest of the figures; compositionally the horse and rider fit into the space perfectly, making them tangential to Victorine; this adds to the impression that both figures are situated on the same plane; the vapid stare of the model is intentional because it suggests that the observer is within the picture plane

2. Edouard Manet, Mlle. Victorine in the Costume of an Espada, *1862. Oil on canvas, 65 x 50¼". Metropolitan Museum of Art, New York. Bequest of Mrs. H. O. Havemeyer, 1929. H. O. Havemeyer Collection.*

The conscious process of dropping or modifying signifiers begins with Edouard Manet's painting. The artist's desire to put down in a few strokes what was before his eyes marks the end of the artist's reign solely as an interpreter of events external to himself. By calling attention to the painting act and its taken-for-granted conventions, Manet is simply proclaiming that *he* is the real subject of his work.

From Manet to Pollock, and until the present, it has been the artist's task to systematically reject or modify signifying conventions so that they may have meaning for a new esthetic context. It is up to each artist to reorganize his signifying systems so that their elements stand in greater distinction or opposition to one another. For example, in the above painting Manet tends to eliminate color by substituting neutral values for dark and light contrasts. This naturalizes the cultural by demonstrating that the painter has volition over his subject; at the same time it culturalizes the natural by imposing a new system over the domain of local color in real environments. Logically the reduction of systematic relationships in pictorial illusionism proceeds by the following steps:

1. Homogenized brushstrokes are made progressively more discrete and tactile (Impressionism, Post-Impressionism, Expressionism, Abstract Expressionism, and so on)
2. Painters steadily reduce depth of field and perspective space
3. Elements are depicted with fewer shadows and less modeling
4. In the evolution toward no color, various symbolic or synthetic color systems are substituted for natural coloration
5. Abstract and then nonobjective forms are gradually substituted for mimetic or illusionistic form
6. In the later stages of abstraction, figure-ground relationships tend to disappear as the picture plane becomes undifferentiated (also referred to as "all-over composition")
7. Physical disruptions begin to be used to redefine the two-dimensional picture plane (Duchamp's mural *Tu M'*, Rauschenberg's combine paintings, and Stella's shaped canvases are notable examples)

Structurally, Manet presents contrasting sets of anti-illusionistic devices.

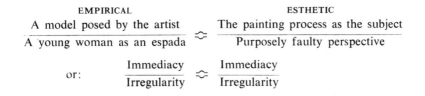

3. CLAUDE MONET: Haystack, Winter, Giverny (1891)

NATURAL	CULTURAL
A haystack near Monet's home in Giverny, at dawn; the snow appears to be melting on the ground; the hill and trees in the background are a medium to dark sky blue	Monet chooses to paint a single haystack at a *specific* location and time of day; this is one of at least thirty in a series of haystack paintings, each recording one of the four seasons according to landscape changes and angle of the sunlight on objects; these paintings focus on a single instant of an illuminated space where sunlight envelops form
Monet's technique is essentially optical and intuitive; he wants to capture what other painters have missed in color-light nuances; the comma-like brushstroke is freer than that used in the landscapes of the 1880's; the snow is bluish white with hints of terra-vert green; the sun remains below the skyline and radiates a warm yellow; the haystack, thinly painted a luminous reddish brown, is in the shadow of the sunlight, in contrast to the coldness of the snow	For Monet distinctions in nature between color and form do not exist; this composition consists of a few relatively simple areas which are basically differentiated by color; the haystack is a light modulator, a neutral architectonic form rather than a bit of rustic scenery; Monet's canvases are the distillation of an experience in seeing rather than the depiction of a landscape for itself
The painting *Haystack, Winter, Giverny*	The "content" of this painting is the artist's translation of atmospheric light into paint pigment
Émile Zola, Antonin Proust, and Theodore Duret are early writers and supporters of Impressionism; subsequent scholars include John Rewald and George Heard Hamilton	Ideologically, Impressionism is a continued reaction against academic tradition through prismatic color, outdoor painting, and natural subject matter

3. Claude Monet, Haystack, Winter, Giverny, *1891. Oil on canvas, 25¾ x 36½". Courtesy, Art Institute of Chicago. Mr. and Mrs. Martin A. Ryerson Collection.*

Claude Monet made his first sizable sum of money when fifteen of the haystack paintings were exhibited at the Durand-Ruel Gallery in 1891. It seems obvious that the artist preferred to have his painting series seen as a group. Monet is emphasizing the *effect of light* on a subject, not the subject itself. Normally, we take for granted the light that surrounds an object. Only by capturing the same object under a number of atmospheric conditions can Monet convince us that light and light reflection is his true goal. *Haystack, Winter, Giverny* is unusual in one respect: the artist uses considerable earth color to back-light the shadow, with smaller amounts of blue and red. The structural equation of Monet's painting continues the painterly literalism begun with the English naturalists.

EMPIRICAL		ESTHETIC
A scene chosen for a series of paintings	·	The fleeting impression of outdoor light rather than a scene
A common outdoor motif as a study in light conditions	≂	White and the spectral colors as pigment equivalents of light

4. GEORGES SEURAT: Evening, Honfleur (1886)

NATURAL	CULTURAL
From a sketch made of the beach near Honfleur and the mouth of the Seine River at sunset	Seurat chooses to make a seascape painting from a series of sketches of the Honfleur area; this is at a point when he is developing Neo-Impressionist theory to a new level of precision and quasi-scientific clarity; the dot brushstroke is used as a dominant element for the first time; color is orchestrated into a mood compatible with other elements in the composition
Evening, Honfleur shows a new uniformity in the use of the divisionist painting technique; although the composition is a study of green-yellow and violet-blue in dominant opposition, Seurat mixed at least 25 different tones to complete the entire painting; the dot technique is built upon a tan-brown underpainting, with freer strokes found in the sky and tighter superimposed dots, mainly of blue and shades of light red, in the lower foreground; the optically devised painted frame which is designed to give every area bordering it optimum brilliancy is a notable innovation	Several critics have mentioned the calmness, almost sadness, of this painting, which is exactly in keeping with Seurat's adopted theory that horizontal lines produce calmness; moreover, the slight downward incline of the pilings produces a hint of sadness; the composition is exquisitely balanced to produce the strongest oppositions between pictorial elements: vertical pilings play against the horizon line, the white reflection of the sunset is set against the jagged rock in the right foreground, while the bluish-yellow sky and water contrast to the bluish-violet of the beach; the allover effect is one of great staticity and forethought (paralleling the stability of Poussin's devices)

4. Georges Seurat, Evening, Honfleur,
1886. Oil on canvas, 25¼ x 31½".
Collection, Museum of Modern Art,
New York. Gift of Mrs. David M.
Levy.

Because Neo-Impressionism appeared to be a precisionist revolt against the romantic carelessness of Impressionist painting technique, it would seem that it actually was "scientific," as some of its advocates claimed. However, in retrospect it appears that the Pointillists were actually fulfilling one of the possibilities opened but not exploited by Impressionism. This was to heighten the retinal illusion of pure light through painting. The Impressionists approached this effect through the contrast of white and primary colors. Georges Seurat methodically produced combinations of contrasting colors which caused the sensation of optical vibration. Seen from the correct distance, each area of *Evening, Honfleur* appears to dance and shimmer in muted fashion. The artist is careful to stabilize his compositions so that they do not conflict with the optical surface of the picture plane. Within a few years, though, the Nabis and later the Fauves would create color contrasts of considerably greater optical violence. Seurat's mature esthetic was published in a newspaper in April or March, 1890. In terms of explicit rules, possibly no major artist has ever committed himself to a clearer statement of intentions.

> Art is harmony; harmony is the analogy of opposites, the analogy of similar elements—of value, of hue, of line; value, that is, light and dark; hue, that is, red and its complementary green, orange and its complementary blue, yellow and its complementary violet; line, that is, directions from the horizontal. These diverse harmonies are combined into calm, gay, and sad ones; gaiety of value is the light dominant; of hue, the warm dominant; of line, lines rising above the horizontal; calmness of value is the equality of light and dark, of warm and cool for hue, and the horizontal for line. Sadness of value is the dark dominant; of hue, the cool dominant; and of line, downward directions. Now, the means of expression of this technique is the optical mixture of values, of hues, and their reactions (shadows), following very fixed laws, and the frame is no longer simply white, as in the beginning, but opposed to the values, hues, and lines of the motif (Homer, pp. 185–86).

Structurally, Seurat continues the use of AIR as the logic mode usually defining figurative art.

EMPIRICAL		ESTHETIC
$\dfrac{\text{The physiological effect of light on the retina}}{\text{A serene seascape}}$	$\backsim$	$\dfrac{\text{The optical sensation of a sunset in divisionist technique}}{\text{The application of discrete dots of colored paint}}$
or: $\dfrac{\text{Physical theory}}{\text{Phenomenal theory}}$	$\backsim$	$\dfrac{\text{Optical sensation}}{\text{Plastic reality}}$

5. PAUL GAUGUIN: THE SPIRIT OF THE DEAD WATCHING (1892)

Gauguin is compelled to paint his mistress who is lying alone in his cabin. Tehura is a young Maori girl terrified of the dark. She mistakes Gauguin's outline in the doorway for an evil spirit. The artist interprets this spirit as an old woman, a symbol of death which he thinks Tehura can understand. Psychologically both women represent *animae,* female figures representing aspects of the artist's unconscious—specifically the tension between carnality and death. Gauguin's title for this work, *Manaõ Tupapaú,* literally means "thinking" and "spirit" with no distinction as to whether the girl or the spirit is doing the thinking. For the painter the old woman signifies transcendency over death; thus the end of lust, while the young girl is sexuality without sin or attachment. The clashing colors surrounding the two figures may define Gauguin's guilt-ridden relationships with women of his own race. At this time his compositions become less angular, the forms softer and larger, and the color applied in ungraduated contrasts. Here he uses a combination of greenish yellow, violet, blue, and yellow-orange which to him connotes a savage, eerie light; the girl's copper-colored skin pulls these colors together, implying sensuality and resolution to an otherwise disharmonious scheme.

5. Paul Gauguin, The Spirit of the Dead Watching, *1892. Oil on canvas, 28¾ x 36¼". Collection, Albright-Knox Art Gallery, Buffalo, New York. A. Conger Goodyear Collection.*

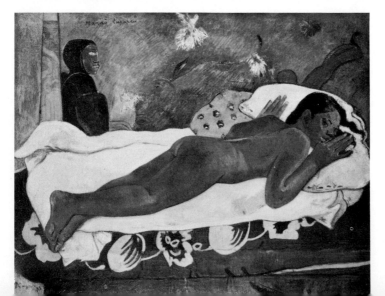

The Spirit of the Dead Watching reveals the inadequacy of formalist criticism. Most critics are content to describe the painting in terms of its composition and to quote Paul Gauguin's letters on its symbolist implications. But clearly the two aspects have to be brought together. To repeat Lévi-Strauss's argument, myths are logical systems that reconcile contradictory factors in man's physical or psychological environment. Art mediates the most fundamental of all predicaments: contradiction between the instinct for survival or immortality and the realization of death's inevitability. Art reduces the physical flow of temporal events to a mental instant, a frozen conceptual order which remains in effect as long as the painting itself.

This painting contains two kernel structures, therefore relating it to the logic of FIRE. FIRE is the preferred form in ritual, myth, and art because it deals with the essence of religious thought, which is the conceptual reconciliation of all the important ambiguities in human culture: life and death, day and night, hot and cold, health and sickness, love and hate, food and famine, etc. Here Gauguin deals with one of the epic Freudian conflicts, the personal battle in each individual between *eros* and *thanatos,* or the desire for gratification and self-destruction.

	EMPIRICAL		ESTHETIC
	The artist's conflict between *eros* and *thanatos*	$\eqsim$	Visual sexual stimulation
	A nude girl having fears of death		The warm brown of the girl's body contrasted to colder surrounding colors
and:	Sexual guilt and death-wish	$\eqsim$	For the artist death's symbolism is sexuality
	Two women *animae* (the conflicting unconscious)		Disharmonious and clashing colors surrounding the body of the girl

71

6. PAUL CÉZANNE: The Basket of Apples (1890–94)

NATURAL	CULTURAL
The motif consists of two horizontal planes, a basket of apples with some apples placed in the foreground, a wine bottle, a tablecloth, and a dish of pastries	Cézanne chooses to paint a still-life which he has organized with extreme care and deliberation; the objects are painted with as much substance and solidity as possible in what Cézanne feels is a revival of Classicism; he "humanizes" his objects by making them the obvious results of his own hand which in itself is a natural response to the structure of nature, thus his remark: "Art is harmony parallel to Nature"
Cézanne organizes the lines of his composition in terms which he feels to be "structural"; in effect this makes the shapes of objects and object relationships geoemetrically consistent with the flat picture plane; the artist's colors are "modulated" so that many shades of the same color are mixed and applied separately in discrete strokes; such incremental adjustments to neighboring colors allow the viewer to sense differences between applied colors and optical gradations on real objects; the later still-lifes and landscapes are painted rather thinly in some areas, preserving the architecture of the brushstrokes and often leaving areas of canvas bare	The obvious visual response to this still-life is not so apparent now as it was when Cézanne painted it; not only is he forcing us to reexamine the physicality of the motif through minor adjustments between objects (for example, the angle of the basket is accommodated by the two table levels and the tilt of the wine bottle, and also the apples are positioned in regard to their effect on their backgrounds), but he is also demanding that we acknowledge the picture plane as a real entity covered with colored brushmarks

6. *Paul Cézanne,* The Basket of Apples, *1890–1894. Oil on canvas, 25¾ x 32". Courtesy, Art Institute of Chicago. Helen Birch Bartlett Memorial Collection.*

Paul Cézanne is possibly the first painter to have examined the implications of a "literalist" picture plane, that is, a pictorial surface that claims no innate powers of illusion but depends upon the ordinary consistency of paint application to provide the naturalistic metaphor. Cézanne is saying that there are only colors of paint: "There are no lines, no forms, but only contrasts."

The structure of Cézanne's art is entirely predictable:

EMPIRICAL		ESTHETIC
To reproduce nature, not to represent it		Cézanne stresses the "arranged" quality of his compositions
The physical substance of the motif	≃	Cézanne reveals a painting to be merely paint and canvas

73

7. PABLO PICASSO: DANIEL-HENRY KAHNWEILER (1910)

NATURAL	CULTURAL
Daniel-Henry Kahnweiler and surroundings	Picasso chooses to paint a portrait of his dealer Kahnweiler
In this painting Picasso gives up his analytic style of faceted outlines for a new conception of space in which large linear planes constantly interrupt the contours created between space and objects; the artist alternately draws and paints, each emphasizing the other; color is used sparingly since it produces illusions of varying depth and a very shallow background is indicated here; generally colors are limited to browns, grays, black and white; Picasso uses flat, discrete brushstrokes (almost like brickwork) to remind us that these are painted surfaces; reflected light seems to have more to do with the painted planes than the space inhabited by the figure	Rather than give us several views of the same person, Picasso suggests the fusions of views between movements by the subject; also Picasso's idea of identifying objects through unique characteristics reminds us that we remember objects through such characteristics regardless of how many different ways we see the objects; thus Picasso paints only those traits which, if omitted, would make an object unrecognizable; for Kahnweiler's portrait these include the subject's hands, watch chain, and much of his face; to the left on a table is a bottle and above that a wooden sculpture from New Caledonia mounted on the wall
The cubist painting *Daniel-Henry Kahnweiler*	The "content" of this painting is the tension between those identifying vestiges of Kahnweiler and cubist painting technique itself
There are many able apologists for Cubism including Kahnweiler himself, Jean Metzinger, Albert Gleizes, Maurice Raynal, André Salmon, and Guillaume Apollinaire	Cubist ideology takes many forms and purposes but its chief goal is to completely eliminate Renaissance form and space

Pablo Picasso's paintings of the 1910–1912 period are nearly without recognizable subject matter and, semiologically, the closest Picasso ever comes to producing a metalanguage system. All metalanguage systems imply that a viewer must be familiar with the ideological argument behind a painting before the work itself can be fully appreciated. To some extent this is certainly true of Cubism. Structurally Picasso is completing a tendency, begun by Manet, which involves heightening the conflict between subject matter and painting technique to the point where the former concedes to the latter.

$$\frac{\text{Picasso selects}}{\text{Physical consistency of}} \underset{\text{the human subject}}{\overset{\text{EMPIRICAL}}{}} \simeq \frac{\text{The fusion of geometry with}}{\text{Material consistency of the painting}} \underset{\text{technique}}{\overset{\text{ESTHETIC}}{}}$$

EMPIRICAL   ESTHETIC

Picasso selects   The fusion of geometry with

Kahnweiler as a subject   personal characteristics of subject

———————————— ≏ ————————————————

Physical consistency of   Material consistency of the painting

the human subject   technique

8. GEORGES BRAQUE: Le Courrier (1913)

*8. Georges Braque, Le Courrier, 1913.
Collage, 20 x 22½". Philadelphia Museum of Art. A. E. Gallatin Collection.*

While Analytical and Hermetic Cubism depend upon essential details, Synthetic Cubism represents objects by juxtaposing real materials or objects with drawn and painted contexts for them. Historically, George Braque's *Le Courrier* upsets the concept of the two-dimensional pictorial object by employing subject matter in three forms: materials representing themselves, materials defining one quality of something else, and drawings *representing* an object or a characteristic of an object. For real materials, the artist chooses strips of paper with simulated wood grain, a single piece of wallpaper, a used tax stamp from a tobacco container, and a portion of the masthead from the newspaper *Le Courrier*. Before gluing down these materials, Braque carefully organizes them on a board painted white. The superimposed charcoal drawing does not conform to the shapes of the glued papers. In fact, different elements of the drawing suggest that we are looking down on the table, viewing it both in elevation and in plan.

Depending upon whether we focus our attention upon the drawn elements or the literal materials, the structure of the *papier collé* fluctuates. Consequently, *Le Courrier* has an intentional double structure represented as FIRE.

	EMPIRICAL		ESTHETIC
	To produce		Materials glued flat
	a still-life of everyday objects		imply more than one perspective
	Table with glassware, tobacco tin, newspaper, etc.	$\backsim$	Glued materials representing themselves
	To produce		Superimposed
and:	a still-life of everyday objects		and conflicting perspective
	Table with glassware, tobacco tin, newspaper, etc.	$\backsim$	Objects drawn with charcoal in the context of glued materials

9. RAYMOND DUCHAMP-VILLON: The Great Horse (1914)

Raymond Duchamp-Villon's *The Great Horse* appears to have been more under the influence of the Futurist's concern with time and speed than of the planar articulations of Cubism. Positions of the horse suggest a set of multiple perspectives which are a metaphor for the passage of time and perhaps for cultural change itself. These suggestions are synthesized into a series of unwinding but integral images, somewhat like Boccioni's *Development of a Bottle in Space* (1912). Since the horse is a prime representation of the shift from animal power to machine power, this work depicts technological flux itself, rather than any specific animal. Here the horse is the icon of a passing age. This tentative casting, made after the artist's death, evolved from a series of small horse and rider studies showing the horse rearing on two feet. Gradually these became the basis for the geometrical horse without a rider.

9. Raymond Duchamp-Villon, The Great Horse, *1914. Bronze (sixth of six casts), 39⅜ x 24 x 36". Courtesy, Art Institute of Chicago.*

Parts of *The Great Horse,* particularly the legs and the hooves, are transformed into geometric forms: pistons and housings, drive shafts and machine cowls, etc. Sharp rectilinear surfaces are played off against gently rounded forms. The original plaster by Duchamp-Villon was later enlarged under his brother's supervision. Before his death in the First World War, the artist hoped to achieve a final version in polished steel.

Cubism is an esthetic of simplification and implication. *The Great Horse* uses the simplifying techniques of Cubism to produce an idea which is neither an "equestrian machine" nor a "mechanized horse," but rather a synthesis of both. As an esthetic Cubism could never function with no subject matter without becoming something else; Robert Delaunay's philosophy of color (Orphism) did move into nonobjective art from Cubism. As with all art, Cubism seeks something beyond itself. For Duchamp-Villon cubist technique provided the means of simulating culture in transition. Again, this sculpture reveals the double structure of FIRE.

	EMPIRICAL		ESTHETIC
	The artist selects the equestrian motif as best summarizing change		The horse's features are nearly lost in the final version
	$\overline{}$	$\backsim$	$\overline{}$
	A horse with machine-like parts		A progressively geometricized horse emerges from earlier models
and:	The artist selects the equestrian motif as best summarizing change		The machine does not appear functional nor do its parts logically relate
	$\overline{}$	$\backsim$	$\overline{}$
	A horse with machine-like parts		The artist depicts a coiled asymmetrical machine in tension

10. WASSILY KANDINSKY: Black Lines (1913)

NATURAL	CULTURAL
Kandinsky's paintings of this period use pictorial elements as complex as those in representational art; technically, he *seems* to be making figurative images, yet real figurative elements are missing.	By 1913 Kandinsky begins to formulate intuitive rules for the use of different forms and colors; this includes specific notions about their emotional meanings; he also produces programmatic analyses of his major compositions implying that there is a readable temporal scheme to his painting similar to music; all of this coincides with the artist's intention of making nonobjective art as concrete as possible
The painting *Black Lines*	*The "content" of* Black Lines *is translatable in terms of the artist's many explanations of color and form; for instance, he states that "Yellow and blue move in opposite directions, gray is stationary"; many of his interpretations are derived from Theosophy and also early studies in perceptual psychology; while* Black Lines *may be interpreted through Kandinsky's many cues, all interpretations remain necessarily personal and vague; all analyses generate emotional correspondences—if the viewer believes in the denoted content of the work*
Although Kandinsky wrote continuously throughout his professional life, Concerning the Spiritual in Art *(1912) and his* Grammar of Creation *(1914) remain the two essays that best direct the serious art student to what the artist wanted his audience to believe about his painting at that time*	The spiritual impulses within modern man account for the urge to make nonobjective art; oppositions within such paintings denote the range of human emotions and degrees of expression; a painter's plastic rhythms correspond to the inner harmonies found in the artist, or lacking in him

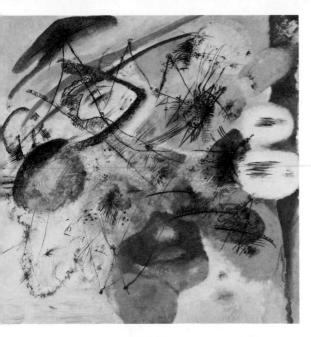

10. *Wassily Kandinsky,* Black Lines,
1913. Oil on canvas, 51¼ x 51¼".
Collection, Solomon R. Guggenheim
Museum, New York.

Wassily Kandinsky's first nonobjective period from 1911 to 1914 includes an initial attempt to justify art exclusively in terms of ideological statements. In 1912 Kandinsky's treatise *Concerning the Spiritual in Art* received much attention as a polemic directed against objective appearances in art. By proclaiming the bankruptcy of scientific materialism, he maintained that art was preparing for a new era of spiritual and visionary expression. He predicted that depiction of the object would be gradually superseded by the creation of abstract elements, divorced from material reality but not separate from the emotional range of the human soul.

Kandinsky's paintings are constructed programmatically according to certain temporal priorities of visual perception, or at least this is the theory. He relates why in his essay "Reminiscences":

> I felt that his [Rembrandt's] pictures "last a long time," and explained it to myself that I had first to exhaust one part continuously and then the other. Later I understood that this division magically produces on the canvas an element which originally seems foreign and inaccessible to painting time (Herbert, p. 29).

Structurally, all nonobjective works such as *Black Lines* reflect the consistency of AIR. Therefore the *empirical sign* for this painting shifts from the missing Plane of Expression to the Connotative Plane above it.

EMPIRICAL		ESTHETIC
Content is defined by the artist's statements and the viewer's feelings		The artist's interpretation of various combinations of forms and colors
The painting as an object	≂	The range of formal elements used by the artist

81

11. MARCEL DUCHAMP: Box in a Suitcase or Valise (Boîte-en-Valise) (1941/42) (1961 edition)

11. Marcel Duchamp, Box in a Suitcase or Valise (Boîte-en-valise), *1941/1942 (1961 edition). 68 reproductions of works by Marcel Duchamp, green clothbound board box, 16 x 14¾ x 3⅛". Collection, Solomon R. Guggenheim Museum, New York.*

The *Boîte-en-valise* is particularly interesting because it appears to be completely culturalized. Marcel Duchamp selects sixty-eight pieces from his total output. Some of these are miniaturized and the rest made into prints. The works fit into a box, and the box may be carried in a valise. In effect, none of the activities suggests naturalizing the cultural except for one: the selection of sixty-eight works of art. The sixty-ninth of course is the idea of the *Boîte-en-valise* itself, except that its structure does not allow it to be art. But here is Barthes's zero degree of opposition, where absence becomes a missing term filled in by implication. Duchamp, however, does imply a natural opposition, naturalizing the cultural through the human sexual implications of the missing sixty-ninth work of art.

11A. FOUNTAIN (AN ASSISTED READY-MADE) (original 1917)

NATURAL	CULTURAL
A urinal turned up on its back and signed "R. Mutt 1917"	Just as nonobjective art *appears* to have content, this assisted ready-made is referred to as a "Fountain" while in reality it is simply a urinal placed somewhat out of context
A mass-produced porcelain urinal	*The "content" of* Fountain *is in the artist's incredible title suggesting that the work in question is some kind of modernist sculpture involving projections of water*
Duchamp's totally enigmatic writings on the ready-mades and related art	Even to critics such art is considered illogical and nonsensical

EMPIRICAL		ESTHETIC
		A urinal is
A urinal designated as a fountain		given an ambiguous context
$\overline{\text{A standard urinal}}$	$\backsim$	$\overline{\text{A slightly modified urinal}}$

The uniqueness of Marcel Duchamp's mature art resides in the fact that it is meant to be a semiotic explanation of all possible types of art. Since *Fountain* is an assisted ready-made, its structure does not refer to AETHER but, instead, to AIR. It operates purely as a modified object with a content defined through a metalanguage explanation. Duchamp's notes for his famous experiment of 1914, *The 3 Standard Stops,* reveal that this piece functions in much the same way as does *Fountain.* It consists of three templates taken from patterns made by three linen threads held out horizontally at arms' length at a height of one meter from the floor and allowed to drop. Each falls, "twisting *as it pleases."* Above the note is the title, *"the Idea of the Fabrication,"* which means this: Duchamp realizes that art at the most extreme stage of nonobjectivity is a matter of letting common materials fall randomly; the content of all nonobjective art is seemingly the making process itself. *The 3 Standard Stops* is an elegant way of creating nonobjective art through the least possible work. In this instance the artist is not only dealing with the effects of randomness, but with these effects incorporated into a *set of elements,* namely the variations on the three threads.

The true ready-mades by Duchamp are few in number and, of course, use the structure of AETHER. First, these are merely chosen, not made. They possess no temporal element as provided by the making process. In his notes for the ready-mades Duchamp insists that one should plan for the specific time to inscribe such a work, waiting, if necessary, for the esthetic response ("with all kinds of delays"). He further insists that the timing in choosing the object is crucial: "—Naturally inscribe that date, hour, minute, as *information* on the ready-made." As a conceptual work *Fountain* has no duration *except* for the time it takes to turn it on its back. In his notes in *The Green Box* Duchamp supplies this observation:

The Clock *in profile*
and the *Inspector* of Space.

NOTE: When a clock is seen from the side (in profile)
it no longer tells time.
MD 58
(Duchamp, Hamilton, and Hamilton)

In effect Duchamp is using a metaphor to explain that the structure of the ready-made negates the effects of time (through the making process) and automatically substitutes the idea of a specific space or art context as a means of defining the art status of the object in question. The true ready-made (AETHER) is always a manufactured, utilitarian object that synthesizes the "sacredness" of FIRE with the "profane" and "natural" quality of AIR and EARTH. In other words, depending upon the circumstances, a ready-made could be used as a tool or functional object or it could be regarded as a symbol of various religious relationships.

11B. BOTTLE DRYER (A TRUE READY-MADE) (original 1914)

NATURAL	CULTURAL
The water attached to the bottles of a bottle rack	The artist *chooses* a utensil which inherently balances the four elements: FIRE, WATER, AIR, and EARTH; intention here is connected to the sacred implications of wine
By hermetic definition the bottle dryer's function is naturally art since it uses a mass-produced metal object (EARTH) *to evaporate* (WATER) *air* (AIR) *from wine bottles* (FIRE)	Equilibration of the Four Principles

12. KASIMIR MALEVICH: Suprematist Composition (Airplane Flying) (1914)

NATURAL	CULTURAL
The artist paints his compositions with a minimum of brushwork and texture; visually his configurations are separated by color, massing, size, and the proximity or overlapping of groups of elements	The interaction of geometric elements in this painting is the result of "economic geometricism" (the artist's term for the field principles of Gestalt psychology)
The artist paints his compositions with a minimum of brushwork and texture; visually his configurations are separated by color, massing, size, and the proximity or overlapping of groups of elements	*Very likely the metalanguage content for this painting derives from World War One airplane formations; for the artist the visual dynamics of these elements in space represent the evolution toward pure feeling and utilitarian perfection; the compositions of black, gray, and red on a white field symbolize the new modes of perceptual response coming into use with dynamic and seemingly gravity-free phenomena*
The painting *Suprematist Composition (Airplane Flying)*	
Malevich's extensive writings on the early phases of modern art including Suprematism	The Suprematist ideology is a fusion of post-cubist formalism and dialectical materialism

12. Kasimir Malevich, Suprematist Composition (Airplane Flying), *1914. Oil on canvas, 22⅞ x 19". Collection, Museum of Modern Art, New York. Photograph, R. Petersen.*

From Manet to Picasso, artists progressively culturalized greater and greater portions of the process ordinarily used in viewing reality. Kasimir Malevich in 1913 goes to the extreme by insisting that human beings develop patterns of perception according to the demands of their environment. When new elements are introduced, they upset previous viewing patterns. Suprematist painting, according to Malevich, provides the guide for the reorganization of twentieth century perception, thus readjusting vision to comprehend the new environment as an organized whole.

The Russian Suprematist movement presents an interesting contrast to the Dutch De Stijl movement of a few years later. Vestiges of Renaissance space still linger in Malevich's painting, particularly in his use of overlapping planes and infinitely deep pictorial space. De Stijl's rectilinear consistency with the picture frame represents a plastically more rigorous approach to composition. Malevich's recognition of Gestalt principles, although unmethodical, is enormously sophisticated for the period 1913 to 1918, since his painting *White on White* (1917) was not grasped problematically until at least the 1950's.

Malevich, however, was convinced that within the initial periods of development in Suprematist painting, he had carried two-dimensional art to its limits. In an essay on Suprematist drawing of 1920 he writes, "There can be no question of painting in Suprematism; painting was done for long ago, and the artist himself is a prejudice of the past" (Malevich, Vol. I, p. 127). The artist felt that the imperative of revolutionary politics and technology would shortly subsume art and its influence on people, and in practical terms he was right. His static images allude to speeding airplane formations as a symbol of the values that lie behind Suprematism, representing perhaps the "literalist" esthetic of the future.

Since the logic structure of AIR is present here, there is no Plane of Content in the Real System. Therefore the Connotative Plane becomes its substitute in defining the empirical sign.

EMPIRICAL		ESTHETIC
The interaction of dynamic masses		Perception of Gestalt Field Relationships
The painting as an object	$\backsimeq$	Geometric figures precisely painted on a white field

13. PIET MONDRIAN: Composition 2 (1922)

NATURAL	CULTURAL
Mondrian constructs a painting by using the most reduced and equilibrated plastic elements on a white surface; he emphasizes the temporal act of painting by the use of overlapping black lines and textural differences between the white ground and the rectilinear colored areas; in later paintings he stresses the painted picture plane even further by allowing the surface of the canvas to project beyond the picture frame itself	By a process of perceptual reduction Mondrian systematically separates and distills the plastic elements of painting, gradually reducing such things as natural coloration, perspective, shading, and subjective content; the artist's unavowed intention is to reconcile the barest painterly elements with the rectilinear physicality of the painting or art object; for this he chooses horizontal and vertical black lines of variable widths because of their oppositional force within the normal picture plane; he selects the primary triad of red, yellow, and blue; with these elements he aims at the highest nonobjective synthesis of equilibrium through absolute oppositions
The art object *Composition 2*	*The metalanguage content of this painting is derived through the artist's insistence that equivalency between plastic elements "creates dynamic equilibrium and reveals the true content of reality" (Mondrian p. 53)*
Mondrian's many essays about his painting	The ultimate goal of Neoplasticism is the merger between art and reality

13. Piet Mondrian, Composition 2, *1922. Oil on canvas, 21⅞ x 21". Collection, Solomon R. Guggenheim Museum, New York.*

Very likely no artist other than Piet Mondrian has ever had such a clear conception of the working rules of art nor such a hopeful vision of the world in a post-art condition. Mondrian realized that the process of dropping signifying terms was inevitable: "What is certain is that no escape is possible for the nonfigurative artist; *he must stay within his field and march towards the consequence of his art*" (Mondrian, p. 62). Similarly he advocated as a principle the fact that "progress" in art depends upon increasingly strengthened oppositions within signifiers: "Plastic art affirms that equilibrium can only be established through the balance of unequal but equivalent oppositions. The clarification of equilibrium through plastic art is of great importance for humanity. It reveals that although human life in time is doomed to disequilibrium, notwithstanding this, it is based on equilibrium" (p. 15).

Mondrian was determined to free his canvases from two-dimensional illusionism (particularly by stressing the painted surfaces, occasionally projecting the picture plane in front of the canvas, and by painting the sides of the canvas as continuations of the picture plane). This creates an essential tension, since it follows that the plastic principles employed are similar to but fewer than those used in figurative painting. It is interesting that Mondrian was forced to use a triad to define his color oppositions. In the late 1950's Edwin Land created a theory of red and green as a basic color polarity which would reproduce all other colors. If Mondrian had had this information in the 1920's when he made his decision, would it have made any difference, or is it the admixture of *primary pigmented colors,* rather than spectral colors, which is essential to his selection? The strength of Mondrian's choice in using horizontal and vertical black lines depends upon two factors: the rectilinear format of most of his paintings, and the fact that although we stand vertically, our eyes are positioned perpendicular to the axis of our bodies. This is an irreducible decision which only Frank Stella challenged in his early paintings. Moreover, we can test the validity of Mondrian's decision by comparing the work of the 1920's with the De Stijl paintings of his colleague Theo van Doesburg. Van Doesburg's 45-degree diagonal positioning of all rectilinear forms annuls much of the possible reinforcement created between the edges of the forms and the edges of his canvases. Apparently the 45-degree angle also reduces tension between the horizontal and the vertical so that historically the work is felt to be less "successful" than Mondrian's.

Structurally the over/under relationships of Mondrian's paintings are very clearly articulated in the artist's writings and technical decisions. Moreover, it is this degree of clarity which makes Mondrian's painting so highly valued as art.

Much of Mondrian's authority as an esthetician stems from his long acquaintance with theosophical ideas and his friendships with several thinkers in related branches of occult philosophy. As with Dr. M. H. J. Schoenmaeker's book *Het Nieuwe Wereldbeeld (The New Image of the World,* first published in 1915), which made a lasting impression on the artist, there are attempts in most areas of occultism to reconcile geometry and natural number theory with the spiritual forces of creation, to use mathematics as a link between the material and the spiritual. Just as important perhaps was Mondrian's friendship with the cabalistically inclined merchant, Salomon Slijper. Given that the Cabala is based on the balancing of opposites and the division of civilizations into four worlds of descending spiritual awareness, there are many indications that Mondrian saw his own art as part of this larger scheme. And if we take the origins of Marcel Duchamp's discoveries seriously, there is further proof that the occult sciences retain the secrets of art. Their message is that art as we know it is nearing its end, and that only its complete disintegration can give us the clarity to see life as "art lived." Mondrian expresses a similar thought: " 'Art' is only a 'substitute' as long as the beauty of life is deficient. It will disappear in proportion as life gains in equilibrium" (Mondrian, p. 32). AIR again is the structure controlling Mondrian's mature art.

$$\frac{\text{EMPIRICAL}}{\text{A minimal number of balanced elements derived from figurative art}} \approx \frac{\text{ESTHETIC}}{\text{Plastic elements aligned with the picture plane itself}}$$
$$\text{The painting as an object} \approx \text{Construction of a Neoplastic painting}$$

14. CONSTANTIN BRANCUSI: Leda (1920)

Brancusi retells the myth of Leda and the Swan (Geist, p. 76) by describing Leda *as the swan;* according to the sculptor, as Leda leans back the lines of her body duplicate those of the bird, thus detouring us away from the most obvious reading of the sculpture. Brancusi's first version of Leda is a one-piece marble carving set on a plaster base; at first glance it seems to be positioned on a very secure and stable foundation. The myth of Leda is, in Sidney Geist's terms, "rationalized" into a "quasi-geometric form." In terms of any formal articulation it has only a few details. The tilt of the marble and the precariousness of the triangular appendage extending from the ovoid body exude a sense of apprehension and imminent unreality.

14. Constantin Brancusi, Leda, *1920. Marble on plaster base, 26 x 19" at widest point. Courtesy, Art Institute of Chicago.*

In his excellent book on the artist, Sidney Geist comments on Henri Bergson's possible influence on Constantin Brancusi. Geist quotes a passage from the philosopher's *Introduction to Metaphysics* where Bergson writes: "Philosophers . . . agree in distinguishing two profoundly different ways of knowing a thing. The first implies that we move around an object; the second, that we enter into it" (Geist, p. 147). Later Bergson relates that the first form of knowing is a matter of *analysis*, while the second depends upon *intuition*. Both of these, of course, correspond to Lévi-Strauss's *humanization of natural law* and *naturalization of human actions*. We begin to understand why Brancusi reorganized the myth so that Leda *becomes* the swan. The sculpture is androgynous and consequently unstable, neither one sex nor the other; its acentric center of gravity also makes it unstable physically. In fact, in many sculptures Brancusi places conceptions of subject matter in opposition to formal articulations.

The mystery behind Brancusi's sculpture is concerned with whether his forms are figurative or nonobjective. Each piece has to be examined separately, but in the case of *Leda* it seems safe to say that the sculpture is nonobjective. Its metalanguage content is the form of the myth itself. But just as important, representation of the characters has been distorted and displaced to the point where mimetic identification is *not* possible *without* reference to the myth. Thus the empirical sign is taken over by the Plane of Connotation.

EMPIRICAL		ESTHETIC
The myth interpreted by Brancusi		The opposition of interpenetrating forms
The sculptured object (off balance)	⌣	Brancusi creates an unstable sculpture

or:

Fusion (conceptual)		Fusion (perceptual)
Instability (physical)	⌣	Instability (physical)

15. NAUM GABO: COLUMN (1923)

NATURAL	CULTURAL
The artist fabricates a construction which appears to be made industrially; its basic form is composed of two sheets of plexiglas intersecting at right angles; its lower superstructure consists of several elements in colored plexiglas arranged according to De Stijl principles	Constructivist sculpture derives its esthetic from the same source as Suprematism, namely the theory of Gestalt perception; in these and other constructions Gabo deals with suspension and tension between forms, transparency and overlapping forms, juxtaposition and symmetry
The construction *Column*	*In "content" this construction is neither abstract nor nonobjective but a reality in and of itself, according to Gabo.* Column *is a unique structure in the same way a new invention or engineering feat is in using principles of engineering economy*
Gabo's and various critics' essays on the Constructivist movement	Constructivism is an esthetic ideology which attempts to integrate modern technical and scientific conceptions of reality with art, demonstrating that both are fundamentally compatible

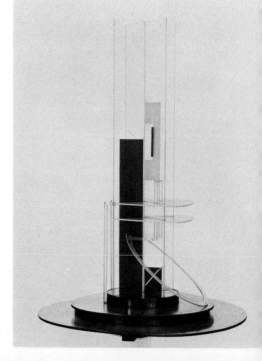

15. Naum Gabo, Column, *1923. Plastic, wood, metal, 41" high. Collection, Solomon R. Guggenheim Museum, New York.*

The early Constructivists advocated motion and time in their work. But with the exception of a few preliminary experiments, these added dimensions were never realized. Yet both Gabo and his brother Antoine Pevsner insisted that their work incorporates a kinetic element. Their reasoning involves the perception of sequential edges and overlapping forms, rather than separate views of a sculptural mass. For mythic structures this is an acceptable temporal element since it in no way affects the duration or coming-into-being of the art object.

Gabo's constructions are successful as art only insofar as they utilize Gestalt principles through geometric relations and he maintains their nonobjective status. The most criticized aspect of Gabo's constructions is his reliance upon engineering and scientific forms. These function as motivated signs on the Plane of Connotation. But as Gabo explains: "It is, therefore, also a mistake to think that when the Constructivist artist uses exact elementary shapes, preferring to draw them with precision which makes them look like geometry, he is by that fact alone trying to make scientific communication. He is not and cannot. My striving to the highest precision of a line or a form or a shape is related to the scientific spirit only insofar as it represents to me the highest and most economic utilization of the pictorial and plastic means for the communication of the image" (Gabo, p. 181).

Thus Gabo's desire to drop the ordinary conventions of sculpture is consistent with but not contingent upon theories of engineering economy and structural elegance. Much of the formal validity of his constructions depends upon their openness and transparency—the "gravity-free" quality that Malevich also sought. Tatlin, as leader of the Productivists in the 1920's, realizing the slight dividing line between constructivist esthetics and modern utilitarianism, chose the latter.

WATER remains the structural matrix for Gabo's art.

EMPIRICAL		ESTHETIC
The column as a unique "invention" of the technical age		The Gestalt qualities of planar and transparent materials
The art object *Column*	≈	The semi-machine-made construction

16. PAUL KLEE: Dance Monster to My Soft Song (1922)

Paul Klee's grasp of the interplay between titles and formal elements in a picture is unequaled. His Bauhaus notebooks (translated into English as *The Thinking Eye*) remain the clearest and most extensive group of theoretical writings on abstract composition. They make it clear that Klee well understood the significance of the Natural-Cultural opposition in works of art. His notes provide numerous working examples of how this dichotomy functions in his own paintings.

Dance Monster to My Soft Song is concerned structurally with the interactions between verbal ambiguity and visual imbalance. Klee decides to make a painting on the theme of marital relationships as seen respectively by both sexes. Semiotically this painting does not fall into any of the normal categories of structural logic. Superficially it resembles FIRE, but on closer examination we find that, while Klee's painting techniques themselves are quite unique, materials and methods have relatively little to do with the structural equation of the work. The fact that the title is a bit of dialogue by the wife forces the work into the realm of cartoon. In other words, the title here is more than description or elaboration; it gives meaning to the painting.

16. Paul Klee, Dance Monster to My Soft Song, *1922. Oil transfer with watercolor on gesso-primed gauze, 14⅛ x 11½". Collection, Solomon R. Guggenheim Museum, New York.*

It should be no surprise that jokes, puns, and other verbal ambiguities are closely related structurally to works of art. Klee's title is meant to be ironic. We get the feeling that the wife's efforts with the player piano and her singing are far from being a "soft song"; instead, there is the implication of something rather shrill and incessant about her overtures. Moreover, the husband is a somewhat docile victim; physically he is large and dominating, but psychologically he remains quiet and unresisting. While the husband commands the center of the composition, the wife in fact dominates the husband. He is quite static, except for a few facial contortions, while she is a spatial disruption. Various off-center features of the husband balance the wife's position in the lower left-hand corner. The word *Ungeheüer* (monster) runs into the music box, perhaps implying that she operates the "monster" just as she does the player piano and the tambourine (or wedding ring) in her other hand. The double structure of this painting deals with two different readings of its Plane of Expression.

EMPIRICAL

ESTHETIC

$$\frac{\text{Klee's notion of how matrimony is seen by each of the sexes}}{\text{Marriage relations}} \approx \frac{\begin{array}{c}\text{"Dance Monster to My Soft Song"}\\ \text{Female skillfully controlling}\\ \text{the unfeeling male}\end{array}}{\begin{array}{c}\text{Drawing of tiny wife physically}\\ \text{dominated by the husband}\end{array}}$$

and:

$$\frac{\text{Klee's notion of how matrimony is seen by each of the sexes}}{\text{Marriage relations}} \approx \frac{\begin{array}{c}\text{"Dance Monster to My Soft Song"}\\ \text{Male puppet dancing to}\\ \text{wife's shrill commands}\end{array}}{\begin{array}{c}\text{Extreme asymmetry of wife}\\ \text{disturbs husband's equilibrium}\end{array}}$$

17. RENÉ MAGRITTE: Song of Love (1948)

Taking into consideration the bland and naturalistic quality of René Magritte's painting, it appears that his particular Surrealism has little to do with technical expressiveness. The transformations involved take place purely on the level of content and are concerned with the logic structure dominated by EARTH. *Song of Love* compels us to deal with apparent contradictions. These logically juxtapose what we know as common knowledge with what we see in the painting. In *Song of Love* there are four triads of contradictory subsets arranged hierarchically. In this instance the center subset of each triad shares at least one conflicting attribute with the two remaining subsets joining it. The logic of these relations has the form of the three-circle Venn diagrams *(a, b, c)* charted on page 59.

We begin with the most general and inclusive contradiction:

1. a. Ships are real   b. Reversal of the natural order   c. Mermaids and mermen are purely fantasy

2. a. Rock is organic   b. Mythical creatures are made of inorganic matter like works of art   c. Mermaids and mermen are mythical beings thought to be made of flesh

3. a. Clouds   b. Negation (silhouette of ship on clouds)   c. Sailing ship

4. a. Humans sing and love   b. Mermaids and mermen can sing and love   c. Fish cannot sing and love

17. René Magritte, Song of Love,
1948. Oil on canvas, 30½ x 38¾".
Collection, Mr. and Mrs. Joseph R.
Shapiro, Oak Park, Illinois.

18. HENRY MOORE: Reclining Figure, II (Two Parts) (1960)

NATURAL	CULTURAL
Since the late 1920's Moore has repeatedly used the theme of the reclining female figure; in fact, it is so implicit that sex does not enter into the title of this work; the reason for the female motif is fairly evident: woman is "natural" according to the Natural-Cultural dichotomy of mythic structures	Moore chooses to sculpt a reclining figure as an expression of a reality running deeper than surface appearances; his aim is to disclose a spiritual vitality based on the close observation of natural forms; this is the basis of the sculptor's espousal of Abstract Vitalism, that the life impulse constantly flows from one source to another (that is, the hand of the sculptor to the sculpture)
Many of Moore's most successful sculptures show a very direct use of sculpture tools (for instance pick hammers that leave unfinished surfaces of jagged plaster or plaster rasps that leave very grainy textures); this figure is cast in two parts simulating perhaps the apparent separateness but underlying continuation of rock strata; here also the "pent-up energy" of the figure is translated through the physical vigor of carving and hammering	In *Reclining Figure, II* there is a very obvious attempt to create a metaphoric union between the condition of human life and the types of gradual erosion that expose sedimentary rock stratifications through thousands of years of exposure to the elements; one implication is that although the time scale may differ vastly, the human body is subject to the same processes of growth, wear, and decay as all natural phenomena; Moore's propensity of playing smooth finished surfaces against extremely rough textures also implies something about the disintegrating state of the sculpture itself: the fact that art changes but remains the same
Moore's statements and particularly the writings of Herbert Read and David Sylvester about the sculptor	Abstract Vitalism needs little explanation since its visual implications are so clearly evident in the sculpture itself

18. Henry Moore, Reclining Figure, II (Two Parts), *1960. Bronze, left: 50 x 34⅝ x 29¼"; right: 36⅝ x 55¼ x 41⅛". Collection, Museum of Modern Art, New York. Given in memory of G. David Thompson, Jr. Photograph, Barrows.*

Through much of Henry Moore's career he has held to the vitalistic metaphor. In the mid- and late 1930's Moore experimented with geometric abstraction, as he did with various forms of surrealist imagery during the 1950's.

EMPIRICAL		ESTHETIC
The reclining female as an archetype of nature		Metaphoric fusion of human life and rock stratification
───────────	≎	───────────
Recovering underlying appearances through vitalism		Simulation of rock surfaces in Moore's sculpting technique

or:

$$\frac{\text{Nature (female)}}{\text{Vitalist metaphor}} \;\approx\; \frac{\text{Human-geological fusion}}{\text{Nature-simulating technique}}$$

19. JACKSON POLLOCK: Cathedral (1947)

NATURAL	CULTURAL
Pollock drips liquid paint from a can or spatters it in long arabesques using a stick; these activities demand total bodily participation; there is a purposeful literality to the materials used in *Cathedral;* they simply represent various kinds of coagulation, liquidity, and absorption (Real System A)	Structurally this painting consists of three connected subsets which comprise a set: the stretchers and canvas, the paints, and the forces of gravity
The above description of Pollock's painting technique (Real System B)	Basically *Cathedral* reads as an object and this remains Pollock's intention
The painting *Cathedral*	*Pollock does not use sketches or preliminary drawings; each painting grows out of a period of purely physical adjustment; the real "content" of Pollock's allover compositions is his ability to remain physically and psychically "in" the work so that a viewer feels that rapport; thus the subject is a direct record of the artist's own mind-body dialogue*
Pollock's few statements and, particularly, the early writings of Clement Greenberg	On the broadest ideological plane Abstract Expressionism represents the transmission of the artist's subconscious impulses through direct, kinesthetic handling of his materials

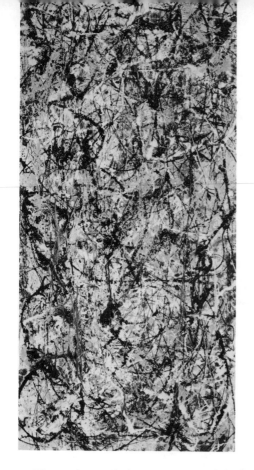

19. *Jackson Pollock,* Cathedral, *1947. Mixed media on canvas, 71½ x 35 1/16". Dallas Museum of Fine Arts. Gift of Mr. and Mrs. Bernard J. Reis, New York.*

The truly revolutionary aspect of Jackson Pollock's art is its negation of the traditional procedure of first designing and then making art. Pollock is undoubtedly a *bricoleur* in Lévi-Strauss's terms, a craftsman who invents in the face of specific circumstances. Moreover Pollock states through his work that conception cannot take priority over the act of creation. At their most inspired, conception and creation stem from each other. Most insistently, he maintained that his compositions were controlled and cerebral—in the sense that all feeling and expression is intellectual: "I don't work from drawings or color sketches. My painting is direct. . . . The method of painting is the natural growth out of a need. I want to express my feelings rather than illustrate them. Technique is just a means of arriving at a statement. When I am painting I have a general notion as to what I am about. I *can* control the flow of paint: there is no accident, just as there is no beginning and no end" (Robertson, p. 194). Thus for Pollock, his state of mind at the time of painting defines the final material object, the painting itself. *Cathedral,* which like Albers's *Homage to the Square* series is structurally defined by WATER and EARTH, signifies the final phases of nonobjective art. It naturalizes materials to a degree only reached by Process Art in the past few years.

20. WILLEM DE KOONING: Woman and Bicycle (1952–1953)

NATURAL	CULTURAL
A woman with a bicycle	De Kooning chooses a woman with a bicycle as a theme for a painting; frequently these are particularly vapid, oversexed females, somehow an obsession to the artist
De Kooning's painting technique grows in ferocity and disregard for the norms of orthodox painterliness; his canvases in the women series show evidence of constantly reworking details; all the mannerisms of past art are magnified into overlapping starts and stops; linework and brushwork fuse in continuous counteraction; contours, figures, and backgrounds are kept purposely vague and incomplete	In spite of his calculated disregard for illusionistic conventions, de Kooning maintains great selective awareness toward color, line, form, and frequently toward specific imagery; although the artist's handling of paint implies a lack of control, his paintings show a clear understanding of cubist space and composition; the violent use of the paintbrush and palette knife seems to be a reaction to the female's real or imagined powers of emasculation—violence acts as a catharsis to the obsession
The painting *Woman and Bicycle*	Some periods of de Kooning's art, such as this woman series, contain recognizable content, others are completely abstract and therefore are metalanguage systems; after 1947 there is little difference between the two so that his nonobjective paintings possess latent content through his figurative work; in both cases, though, content is largely defined through the artist's formal intentions

20. Willem de Kooning, Woman and Bicycle, *1952–1953. Oil on canvas, 76½ x 49". Collection, Whitney Museum of American Art, New York. Photograph, Geoffrey Clements.*

Willem de Kooning's *Woman and Bicycle* represents the link between the limits of Expressionism and its continuation in Abstract Expressionism. Formal organization is necessary and present, but obscured by various painterly abuses to the picture plane. Emotion signified by the making process is carried over into de Kooning's nonobjective painting of subsequent periods. The gathering and release of sexual tension through the act of painting is recapitulated for the art audience by such descriptions as Barbara Rose's:

> De Kooning's pictorial dilemma is spatial. Contours are opened to allow flesh and environment to flow into one another, and anatomical forms themselves have been fragmented: hence there is no clear statement as to where the figure is actually located in space. This ambiguous space de Kooning has referred to as the "no-environment," a metaphor for the dislocated space in which the flux of modern life takes place. Tension then arises out of the difficulty in determining where the figure is placed as it emerges from its chaotic environment to assume its own identity. In the paintings of the early fifties there is a new violence, aggressiveness, and brusqueness of attack as the paint is hurled on the canvas in the heat of execution. Such an attack, in which the loaded brush is allowed to drag and sweep across the canvas trailing meteoric splashes and drips, came to be identified as the characteristic means of execution of gestural abstraction or "action painting" (Rose, p. 184).

"Action" painting thrives on excessive biographical detail, particularly anecdotes and circumstances surrounding the act of painting itself. In the tradition of high romanticism, the title of each painting implies, but rarely reveals, specific emotional attachments. Abstract expressionist titles elaborate emotional associations behind the making process; in Object Art, however, since making is culturalized and subject matter nonexistent, titles are considered misleading and therefore are rarely used. Structurally, Abstract Expressionism depends upon formal resolution of a technically unlimited making process. Such paintings signify "states" of being, both the artist's and the painting's.

EMPIRICAL		ESTHETIC
The subject as a private obsession of the artist which is resolved		The painting formally completed
A woman with a bicycle	$\backsim$	A painting unfinished technically, thus still "alive" in terms of the artist's participation

21. FRANZ KLINE: Mahoning (1956)

NATURAL	CULTURAL
As a rule Kline works on an unstretched canvas tacked to the wall, with house-painting brushes (before he could afford artist's oil paints Kline used house paints); his technique is intentionally meaty and sloppy; the slashing and dragged brush strokes signify involvement and emotion; *Mahoning* uses some brown coloring	Kline's mature painting functions along the lines of basic Gestalt dynamics; to some extent these "balanced" paintings are the result of sketches, although the finished works may change radically from these; the best Klines reduce color and value to black and white contrast and admixtures through overpainting; his art generally evolves through trial and error
The painting *Mahoning*	*The "content" is Kline's painting experience, rather than a form of symbolism or calligraphy; frequently Kline applies simple descriptions or geographic names for titles; these are attached to a painting after it is finished; thus it is significant that most abstract expressionists feel the need to give conceptual content to their works through titles; Kline insists that his paintings have reversible figure-ground relationships, although it is evident in many cases that black is superimposed on white*
Kline's statements are probably the most reasonable and direct of any abstract expressionist	The ideology of Abstract Expressionism attempts to identify the lives and tribulations of its practicing artists with their paintings

21. Franz Kline, Mahoning, *1956. Oil on canvas, 80 x 100". Collection, Whitney Museum of American Art, New York. Gift of the Friends of the Whitney Museum of American Art. Photograph, Geoffrey Clements.*

Franz Kline's painting presents some of the same ambiguity inherent in the structure of Jackson Pollock's art. His making procedure is both planned and unplanned. But while he demonstrates Pollock's spontaneity, the artist tends toward compositional solutions, partly devised and partly accidental. Kline claimed to have rejected the figure-ground concept. Yet nearly always his compositions read as black on white. The tension in his compositions is strongest when Kline works in extreme contrasts. His color paintings and those depending upon gray seem to lack resolution, although some are successful.

Dialectically, the structure of Kline's painting echoes most Abstract Expressionism: it implies a successful conclusion to a painting via formalist criteria through the least traditional control of the painting act. Painting becomes its own subject matter and purpose.

$$\frac{\text{The painting experience}}{\text{The painting } Mahoning} \approx \frac{\overset{\textstyle\text{ESTHETIC}}{\text{Balancing broad}}\;\text{black and white brush strokes}}{\text{A painting generated by emotion which depends upon the most elemental handling of materials}}$$

EMPIRICAL — The painting experience / The painting *Mahoning*

ESTHETIC — Balancing broad black and white brush strokes / A painting generated by emotion which depends upon the most elemental handling of materials

22. JASPER JOHNS: Painted Bronze (1964) (original 1960)

NATURAL	CULTURAL
Two Ballantine beer cans (Real System A)	Johns selects two Ballantine beer cans to be cast; the intention is to transform common objects into art
The cans are cast and set on a bronze plinth	These cans were originally finished in a bronze coating by the manufacturer; Johns's act of casting the cans simply duplicates their natural state as consumer products

22. Jasper Johns, Painted Bronze, *1964 (original 1960). Painted bronze, 5½ x 8 x 4½". Courtesy of the artist. Photograph courtesy Leo Castelli Gallery, New York. Photograph, Rudolph Burckhardt.*

NATURAL	CULTURAL
Two cast beer cans (Real System B)	The artist now intends to transform art into common objects
Johns hand-paints labels onto the cast cans	The labels destroy the integrity of the beer cans as "sculpted bronzes," thus affirming their art quality by making them nonart

Seemingly simple art works frequently contain the most challenging structures. Most of Jasper Johns's sculptures are visual puns on the related consistency of art materials and the physical consistency of the objects used as subjects. *Painted Bronze* is a direct casting roughly finished, just as its label is purposely hand-painted. The art is dependent upon the viewer *knowing* the inversions made by Johns. This double structure, which Johns employs often, is related to the semiotic element FIRE.

Jasper Johns and Robert Rauschenberg are immediate forerunners of Pop Art. There is, however, an underlying difference between the two artists. The structure of Johns's art is frequently concerned with different readings of the same object or device while that of Rauschenberg is more related to juxtaposition and collage. Casting and painting in Johns's work are particularly elegant since, depending upon how a work is interpreted, both acts have naturalizing and culturalizing overtones.

Since 1954 all of Johns's work depends upon a reciprocity between content and handling. Reputedly Johns's first flag painting (1954) was inspired by a dream. Simply presenting the American flag in its iconic, rectilinear form (matching the dimensions of the canvas) is tantamount to culturalizing the natural, while using the painterly encaustic technique naturalizes the flag as a symbol and standardized object. Note Johns's statement: "I try to pick something which seems to me typical, undistinguished by its peculiar aesthetic or design qualities. I am interested in things which suggest the world rather than suggest the personality" (Kozloff, p. 31).

In the *Target with Four Faces* (1955) Johns decided, *subsequent* to painting the target, that he would include a box relief with four life-casts of faces. Johns may have realized that the targets could be interpreted as purely artistic devices. So the faces not only lend a particular kind of vulnerability and tension to the target, they emphasize the contrast between three-dimensional objects and objects such as paper targets and cloth flags that are nominally considered to be two-dimensional. The artist's paintings of this period consistently deal with the ambiguity of three-dimensional objects rendered in an illusional painterly fashion and that same illusionism forced life-size onto the artist's two-dimensional picture plane.

It seems that Johns is particularly aware of the order of inversions. All successful artists using the double structure of FIRE follow a somewhat similar procedure. Johns notes in his sketchbook (Kozloff, p. 40):

> Take an object.
> Do something to it.
> Do something else to it.
> "   "   "   "   "

23. DAVID SMITH: Cubi XXVII (1965)

NATURAL	CULTURAL
The Cubi units are hollow stainless steel boxes and cylinders made by Smith and his assistants; the units are welded together; the final grinding and polishing, done by Smith alone, gives the piece sufficient lightness and unity	This last work in the Cubi series epitomizes Smith's handling of the cubist idiom; it combines massiveness, frontality, openness, and the delineation of planar surfaces—but most importantly the sculpture *appears* precariously balanced as a formalist composition mainly concerned with the periphery of the composition
The fabricated art work *Cubi XXVII*	*Part of the Cubi series revolves around the motif of the gate or arch; visually these portals look unstable and dangerous to pass through; consequently Smith has blocked the entrance to each of them*

23. David Smith, Cubi XXVII, *1965.*
Stainless steel, 111⅜ x 87¾ x 34".
Collection, Solomon R. Guggenheim
Museum, New York.

The structure of David Smith's sculpture never varies; it mirrors the procedures of all pre-Pollock abstractionists. Yet there are elements in his work that connect it with the minimalists of the 1960's. For one, Smith had the habit of collecting odd pieces of metal, saving these until an idea provoked him to juxtapose them to other shapes. Here is Lévi-Strauss's *bricoleur,* who, in activity, falls somewhere between the maker of collages and the selector of ready-mades. Obviously there is a degree of standardization in the elements of Smith's Cubi series, although esthetically and psychologically it would have been impossible for Smith to adopt the "literalism" of Judd's or Morris's work.

With *Cubi XXVII* it is difficult to decide whether the gate theme should be considered content or a metalanguage elaboration upon a basically nonobjective theme. Since the gate theme is introduced into a deliberately nonfigurative series, it seems more reasonable to connect the sculpture with the structure of AIR. Although the forms of the sculpture relate as a total composition, their off-balance assembly gives the work a sense of unstable balance.

$$\frac{\text{EMPIRICAL}}{\underset{\text{The object (physical stability)}}{\text{A gate (conceptual stability)}}} \approx \frac{\text{ESTHETIC}}{\underset{\text{Welding (physical stability)}}{\text{Appearance (balanced instability)}}}$$

24. MORRIS LOUIS: Saraband (1959)

NATURAL	CULTURAL
Louis works with large areas of un-stretched cotton duck; the acrylic paints, both in full strength and diluted, are poured directly on the canvas; the canvas is folded and sloped to control the flow and speed of the paint (Real System A)	Perceptually Louis's canvases remain "unstructured" in the way Pollock's are, yet they have the same subset relations of paint, canvas, and gravity controlling them; while Pollock's canvases seem random, one can usually see a directionality in the flow of paint for Morris's canvases
Same description as above (Real System B)	Basically one reads Morris's paintings as objects with no implied Gestalt defining the picture plane

24. Morris Louis, Saraband, *1959. Acrylic on canvas, 100½ x 149". Collection, Solomon R. Guggenheim Museum, New York.*

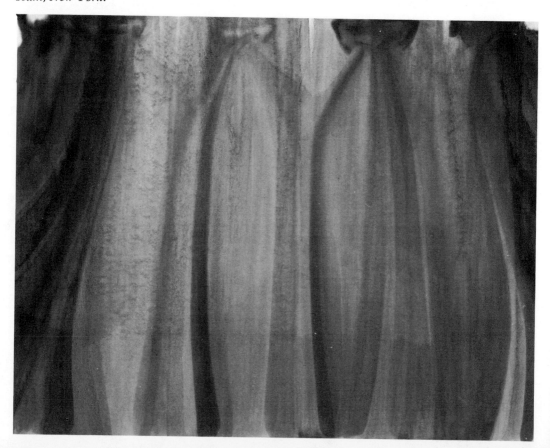

The structure of Morris Louis's painting contains the same ambiguity as Pollock's. For both, materials are self-representative, thus *naturalizing the cultural*. Louis also reverses the making procedure by allowing gravity to direct the flow and saturation of the paint, controlling the paint to some extent by creating valleys, folds, and depressions in the canvas itself. Consequently, the "formal abstractionists" regard Louis as a brilliant colorist and innovator in field composition. On the other hand, some "literalists" or process artists look upon Louis, as they do Pollock, as a logical precursor to their own efforts. For the formalists, Louis's color results from his skill and selectivity in composition. Some "literalists," though, would regard the waves, folds, and overlapping strains in *Saraband* as evidence of a sequential operation, with color as a kind of separator or indicator of the activities themselves.

Within the polemics of art criticism there is a key controversy between "formalists" and "literalists." What both groups do not understand is that the issue is simply a matter of the priorities of artistic transformation. Traditionally so-called modern art has been a matter of choosing an entity as art (culturalizing the natural) and then embellishing it through the artist's personal handwriting (naturalizing the cultural). Minimalists and process artists have sought to reverse this by choosing completely standardized materials or objects (naturalizing the cultural) and articulating these materials through the most reasonable acts and decisions (culturalizing the natural). In this last instance the process is never completely reversed; this was first (and ultimately) accomplished in 1914 by Duchamp with the *Bottle Rack*. Object Art and Process Art can only approximate the conceptual elegance of Duchamp's choice.

All formalist art depends upon the ideological support of writers and critics to give it "meaning" in the art historical context. For color-field painters such as Louis, Noland, Olitski, and Frankenthaler this has happened through the very able writings of Clement Greenberg, William Rubin, Lawrence Alloway, and others. All so-called "literalist" art depends just as much on verbal or written justification, but the problem increases as such art moves away from the approved canons of formalist theory. New esthetics for "literalist" tendencies have to be found. Ironically the various forms of drip and stain painting are very much "literalist" efforts, yet this has never bothered those critics who have attacked Object Art and Process Art. As in Pollock's work, Louis's painting contains the double structure of EARTH and WATER—on an allegorical level WATER represents the return of all semiotic structures to their most naturally fluid and unmanipulated consistency.

Depending upon how one interprets Frank Stella's *Newstead Abbey*, it reads either as a "literalist" or a "formalist" painting. Stella's subsequent rejection of the literalist interpretation of his early painting is consistent with his shaped color compositions after 1964. These developed into the brilliant logos of the protractor series starting in 1967, and have since become more and more bounded by a rectilinear format. What is radical about *Newstead Abbey* is that its three-dimensionality reinforces the illusionism of its picture plane, and its painted surface reinforces its objecthood. Irreducibly the painting represents contradictions inherent in all painting—this is the gap between idea and physicality which totemism bridges. *Newstead Abbey* as an esthetic position is a *cul de sac,* so it is not surprising that Stella began to incorporate color and internal composition later on. The choice was between this or working in three dimensions. Quite obviously, by the addition of once-dropped signifiers, Stella repudiated literalism for formal abstraction, reversing his position vis-à-vis Pollock.

Like Albers's painting, Frank Stella's *Newstead Abbey* seems to have the double consistency of FIRE, but it is really the "literalist" structure of AIR and EARTH juxtaposed. On the formal level of AIR the painting reads as an *object,* nothing more. Yet its painting motif is a series of subsets (EARTH) of stripes comprising a single symmetrical figure.

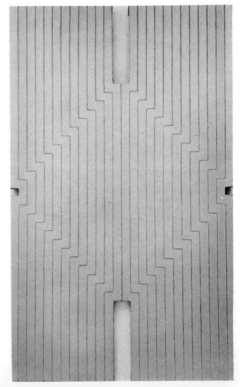

25. Frank Stella, Newstead Abbey, *1960. Aluminum paint on canvas, 120 x 72". Courtesy, Stedelijk Museum, Amsterdam. Photograph, Rudolph Burckhardt.*

NATURAL	CULTURAL
Stella makes a composition based on simple grid principles in which the canvas stretchers, as boundaries, become the motif for the painting itself (Real System A)	On one level *Newstead Abbey* reads as an object; the stretchers, their thickness and role in creating the composition, emphasize the three-dimensional rather than the pictorial nature of the painting.
Stella paints a series of stripes with metalized enamel paint; these are separated by narrow pinstripes of bare cotton canvas (Real System B)	Perceptually, the picture plane creates the ambiguity of whether the painted lines emanate from the cuts made in the stretchers or the stretchers conform to the two-dimensional design
The painting *Newstead Abbey*	*The painting uses a single color, or noncolor, an aluminum paint which Stella maintains simply represents itself, just as Pollock insisted that his paintings were paint*

$$\text{EMPIRICAL} \qquad\qquad \text{ESTHETIC}$$

$$\frac{\text{A nonillusionistic painting}}{\text{The painting } Newstead\ Abbey} \quad \approx \quad \frac{\text{A three-dimensional object}}{\text{Composition defined by canvas stretchers}}$$

and:
$$\frac{\text{A nonillusionistic painting}}{\text{The painting } Newstead\ Abbey} \quad \approx \quad \frac{\text{A diamond (illusion) defined by stripes}}{\text{A series of painted stripes}}$$

26. ANDY WARHOL: Portrait of 16 Jackies (1964)

NATURAL	CULTURAL
Five media photographs of Jacqueline Kennedy (Onassis), using one smiling and four funeral photographs (Real System A)	Warhol decides to make a multiple portrait of a celebrity with as little artistic intervention between the subject and the medium as possible
High-contrast photographs are silk-screened in two colors on canvas with some minor mistakes in the register and texture of the images; there is no attempt here to duplicate the precision and craft of high art graphics	The images of Jackie have no depth or meaning beyond their form as standardized icons employed in selling newspapers and magazines
The photographs of Jackie are a set containing three subsets: a happy portrait, four sorrowful portraits, and Jackie's face as a source of popular emotion (Real System B)	Warhol is giving us Jackie, one of the world's most exploited personalities and stereotypes, as a woman capable of human feelings
Warhol's technique of selection is in itself the creativity of the making process	Through all the loss of detail and intentional banality of the photographs we are forced to see Jackie as a person rather than as an icon

26. Andy Warhol, Portrait of 16 Jackies, *1964. Acrylic and silkscreen enamel on canvas, 80 x 64". Collection, The Museum of Contemporary Art, Nagaoka, Japan. Photograph courtesy Leo Castelli Gallery, New York. Photograph, Rudolph Burckhardt.*

Andy Warhol's culturalization of the natural is fairly sophisticated: for art purposes he duplicates a set of photographs of a famous living person (media photographs of some anonymous person do not carry the same implications of standardization). The photographs, naturalized through printing flaws, are the product of a news-gathering process. Warhol is not adverse to publicizing that he makes endless editions of some of his works; this also acts as a form of naturalization. The artist's genius is in recognizing the totemized environment of brand products and mass media in the way primitives naturally totemize animal species.

Portrait of 16 Jackies deals philosophically with the phenomenon of fame and standardization. Famous symbols are by necessity a combination of the unique and the banal repeated *ad nauseam*. Such popular icons have a wealth of associative meaning and much exposure of their private lives, yet ironically they remain somehow nonhuman, fabricated stereotypes of the media.

EMPIRICAL	ESTHETIC
A "mechanical" interpretation by the artist / Five photographs of Jackie	The images are banal icons / The photographs are reproduced in silkscreen with no thought given to subtleties or technique
Warhol's selection reveals a human being / Jackie in more than one emotional state	In spite of the commonness of the images we see a real person / Here the making process is selection and juxtaposition

While less sophisticated, Warhol's early soup cans adhere to nearly the same formulas. For instance, a single painting or one soup can (or an array of one hundred cans) is made from the advertisement for Campbell's Beef Noodle Soup. Here again it is the standardized types of soup and their endless proliferation that makes them like the silkscreen process.

EMPIRICAL	ESTHETIC
Artist chooses logotype of a name brand / Campbell's Beef Noodle Soup	Both subject and reproduction technique remain the instruments of mass-production / Use of mechanical techniques of advertising

Similarly a universal icon is painted by hand on a canvas as "art." The artist realizes that a standardized product or image of the product is essentially a piece of language containing both syntagm and system; in this case the system is mass-distributed food. Warhol plays one off against the other. His statements necessarily reflect a kind of "irony of indifference" which stresses, for esthetic reasons, that his involvement is always impersonal.

118

The interviewer should just tell me the words he wants me to say and I'll repeat them after him. . . .

The reason I'm painting this way is because I want to be a machine. Whatever I do, and do machine-like, is because it is what I want to do. I think it would be terrific if everybody was alike. . . .

If you want to know all about Andy Warhol, just look at the surface of my paintings and films and me, and there I am. There's nothing behind it. . . .

In the future everybody will be world famous for fifteen minutes.

> (*Andy Warhol* exhibition catalogue, first published for the Museum of Modern Art in Stockholm in 1968)

These remarks reflect on the mechanisms of the post-historical art world; they also reveal why the best Pop artists are strenuously anti-ideological.

27. ROY LICHTENSTEIN: LITTLE BIG PAINTING (1965)

NATURAL	CULTURAL
The reproduction of an abstract expressionist painting (denoting "action" and emotion) (Real System A)	Lichtenstein chooses to duplicate a reproduction of a painting
The artist's version is made by stenciling and hand-painting the image on canvas; this is done either by Lichtenstein or an assistant	The comic strip versions have of course lost the emotional implications of the original; but Lichtenstein maintains that his compositional alterations, as slight as they might be, are a necessary aspect of his "art"
The reproduction of an abstract expressionist painting (denoting "action" and emotion) (Real System B)	Lichtenstein chooses to duplicate a comic book reproduction of a painting
The artist's version is made so literal that it could easily be a blown up photolithographic reproduction	This is not art, but merely a commercial copy of a comic book reproduction

Roy Lichtenstein's art reveals a curious schism between content and intention. Both conception and making are divorced as much as possible from the original intentions of the copied work. Much of this reifies the emotional aridity behind contemporary media.

$$\frac{\text{EMPIRICAL}}{\text{The artist chooses to duplicate a reproduction}}{\text{Reproduction of an abstract expressionist painting}} \rightleftharpoons \frac{\text{ESTHETIC}}{\text{Slight alterations which make Lichtenstein's version "art"}}{\text{The artist's enlarged version}}$$

and:

$$\frac{\text{The artist chooses to duplicate a reproduction}}{\text{Reproduction of an abstract expressionist painting}} \rightleftharpoons \frac{\text{Not art but a commercial copy}}{\text{A literal blowup of the original}}$$

Pop Art has no ideology in the sense that most modernist art movements have. The rationale of much of Warhol's and Lichtenstein's art depends upon the diminishing differences between commercial graphic advertising and so-called high art. It is this lack of difference that provides the ambivalence of FIRE, the either-or connotations necessary for this particular structure. This gives us a clue as to why the paintings and assemblages by James Rosenquist and Tom Wesselmann are esthetically less succinct: both draw on collage and cubist techniques of abstraction, diluting the essential message of Pop Art, namely that everything made today is both art and nonart.

While Lichtenstein considers himself a compositionalist, it is only necessary for the viewer to *know* this. Whether it is true or not makes no essential difference. When Lichtenstein uses comic strip panels and modern "old masters" he is most successful because his work depends upon banal content kept in essentially the same form as the original. His prints, metal-enamel panels, landscapes, and 1930's abstractions are paradoxically less impressive because he alters the original format too much or succeeds in parodying himself.

7. *Roy Lichtenstein,* Little Big Painting, *1965. Oil on canvas, 68 x 80".* *Collection, Whitney Museum of American Art, New York. Gift of the Friends of the Whitney Museum of American Art. Photograph, Geoffrey Clements.*

28. CLAES OLDENBURG: Dormeyer Mixer (1965)

NATURAL	CULTURAL
All Dormeyer mixers of the same model	Oldenburg decides to reproduce a common object
Oldenburg and assistants re-create the mixer in a "soft" version using vinyl, wood, and kapok stuffing	In their own way the materials that Oldenburg uses to make the "soft sculpture" are just as sleazy, common, and impermanent as the appliance he is copying

28. Claes Oldenburg, Dormeyer Mixer, *1965. Vinyl, wood, and kapok, 32 x 20 x 12½". Collection, Whitney Museum of American Art, New York. Gift of the Howard and Jean Lipman Foundation, Inc. Photograph, Geoffrey Clements.*

Claes Oldenburg's constructions employ the same structure as most successful Pop Art. He uses materials and techniques of fabrication which in some sense are commercially analogous to the things he is imitating. Many of Oldenburg's early duplications are rough plaster castings haphazardly painted with glossy enamels. Gradually, though, this approach has been expanded to include enlargement, softness, plastic artificiality, and sexuality in the expression of mass-produced objects, since, latently or not, these are subliminally built into the products anyway.

EMPIRICAL		ESTHETIC
To reproduce		Oldenburg's fabrication has
the everyday environment		the same qualities as the object
A Dormeyer mixer	≈	A mixer made in plastics

George Segal's tableaux demonstrate Pop Art in a somewhat different fashion. Rather than using the elemental structure of AIR as Oldenburg does, Segal's constructions have the quality of the collage and the structure of FIRE. Segal's compositions consist of plaster replicas of real people installed in fragments of actual environments. Thus the cast figures represent live people in real situations. Although the environments are non-living, materially they are more "real" than the figurative castings of real human beings inhabiting them.

29. JEAN TINGUELY: Motor Cocktail (1965)

NATURAL	CULTURAL
A motor, machine components, metal fixtures, and scrap metal	Tinguely decides to make a motorized sculpture
Tinguely creates a sculpture entitled *Motor Cocktail,* which incorporates the figure of a rooster and motions used in mixing a cocktail; the inverted frame of the sculpture further suggests a cock's tail	Mythically there is a fundamental misalliance in the synthesis of a motor and naturalistic imagery; Tinguely however seems unconsciously aware of this and attempts to mediate the difference in various ways: the motor is made an integral part of the work; intentional noise made by parts of the sculpture is a form of "charivari," mediating an abnormal union; and lastly, the motor and connecting parts are defectively constructed so that the motorized life of the sculpture seems limited and provisional

29. Jean Tinguely, Motor Cocktail, *1965. Steel and iron, motorized, 30½ x 24 x 10½". Collection, Mr. and Mrs. Joseph R. Shapiro, Oak Park, Illinois.*

Art can only operate in the mythical dimension of historical time if temporal elements connected to it are made finite. Since all Kinetic Art is only seen and validated *in time,* it never becomes a part of historical time. Jean Tinguely has to some extent overcome this by presenting a motorized formalist sculpture as a misalliance.

This takes the form of exaggerated noise and imminent breakdown. Far less acceptable as art are those kinetic works which employ hidden motors that operate silently. Such devices completely fail to grasp the nature of art, although they may be enjoyable to watch. As Lévi-Strauss indicates (1964, pp. 285–89), noise in a mythic context signifies a reprehensible union (charivari), that is a union of elements (natural, man-made, and biological) which is negative and discontinuous. Noise as such signifies that a mythic arrangement (a motor and a sculpture) does not function according to the rules of mediation. Rotten meat and abnormal marriage are two situations, according to Lévi-Strauss, that are accompanied by a loud din. For most kinetic works it seems unlikely that there can be a successful naturalization of the cultural. Tinguely tries to accomplish this by using various anthropomorphic or animal associations. Most of these, however, are signifiers and usually superfluous to the structural equation of the art itself.

If the preceding is true, what accounts for the enormous artistic success of Alexander Calder's mobiles? The mobiles are successful art because they are designed and constructed to balance in a *static state.* Mechanized sculpture is antigravitational; the mobiles depend upon the stabilizing force of gravitation. Mythically, and hence conceptually, the mobiles are in equilibrium. Their motion is "accidental," the result of forces external to the constructions themselves. We *know* that while in motion the mobiles are seeking rest.

30. BRIDGET RILEY: CURRENT (1964)

The esthetic validity of Optical Art is sometimes questioned because it reveals a strong affinity with standard optical illusions appearing in many books on visual psychology. Therefore "Op Art's" art content has been questioned by not a few critics. The optical ambiguity of Riley's painting does not refer to the structure of FIRE; rather, like the Albers painting, it alludes to synthetic FIRE, the fusion of EARTH and AIR. *Current* deals with a reductivist phenomenon, namely wave-like lines moving in an essentially vertical direction (AIR). A second structure is concerned with two interrelated subsets of black and white lines which, because of their identical nature and direction, produce the illusion of a moving and raised surface (EARTH).

NATURAL	CULTURAL
Lines for this painting are first outlined with a set of parallel markers, and then filled in by hand with black acrylic paint (Real System A)	On one level *Current* can be reduced to three connected subsets: two series of black and white lines and their interrelation through the illusion of a three-dimensional surface
Lines for this painting are painted in as described above (Real System B)	*Current* deals with a simplified Gestalt pattern in which all oppositions are reduced to the vertical dimension
The painting *Current* as an object	*Riley writes that such paintings as* Current *generate a disturbance or "event" in the spectator's mind—out of the latent energies in the forms she is using; the fact that the spectator is encouraged to experience simultaneously "something known and something unknown" may be analogous to the particular double structure of the painting*

0. Bridget Riley, Current, *1964. Synthetic polymer paint on composition board, 58⅜ x 58⅞". Collection, Museum of Modern Art, New York. Philip Johnson Fund. Photograph, R. Petersen.*

31. ELLSWORTH KELLY: Spectrum, III (1967)

NATURAL	CULTURAL
A series of thirteen equal-sized panels: yellow / yellow-orange / orange / red-orange / red / red-blue / violet / blue / blue-green / green-blue / green / yellow-green / yellow (Real System A)	*Spectrum, III* is reducible to three connected subsets of a single set: the painted panels as a series of thirteen rectangular objects, the nondiscrete color spectrum, and the spectrum divided into twelve colors with one panel repeating yellow
A series of thirteen equal-sized panels covered as evenly as possible with twelve synthetic polymer paints (Real System B)	Since *Spectrum, III* is composed of thirteen joined panels, the viewer reads the entire painting as a simple Gestalt series with a horizontal axis

31. Ellsworth Kelly, Spectrum, III, *1967. Synthetic polymer paint on canvas in thirteen parts, overall 33¼″ x 9′ ⅝″. Collection, Museum of Modern Art, New York. Gift of the Sidney and Harriet Janis Collection. Photograph, Mathews.*

During the early 1950's Ellsworth Kelly made paintings of colored squares and various series of solidly painted and joined panels such as *Red Yellow Black White Blue* of 1953. Following this and until the mid-1960's, the artist developed his familiar style of hard-edge composition. These works represent the most extreme reduction of ordinary phenomena to flat juxtaposed shapes, frequently utilizing figure-ground reversals and other optical effects. Kelly's joined panels of the late 1960's, however, transform color itself into latent subject matter. Such paintings, just like Ad Reinhardt's Black Paintings, recognize the fact that abstract composition has reached a point of formal exhaustion. At such a point the double structure of AIR and EARTH takes over.

Kelly's panel paintings and Reinhardt's Black Paintings were anticipated by Marcel Duchamp's work of 1920, *Fresh Widow*. In his semi-ready-made Duchamp recapitulates this particular semiotic structure by producing an object (AIR) which is a miniature French window; the doors have eight lights covered with black leather; therefore the leather squares and French window are subsets interconnected to the eight window panes (EARTH), made opaque. "Fresh Widow" and "French window" combine linguistically to give us an ambiguous mixture.

129

32. DONALD JUDD: Untitled (1967) (Eight Boxes)

NATURAL	CULTURAL
These boxes are fabricated by a shop from plans drawn up by the artist: they are made of cold-rolled steel and painted in lacquer (Real System A)	The boxes reduce sculpture to its most essential component, namely a three-dimensional mass which can be visually conceived without looking at the object itself; the cubes are eidetic images
For all practical and esthetic purposes these boxes are identical fabrications (Real System B)	These eight cubes make up three connected subsets: the cubes themselves, the seven spaces between the cubes, and the rectangular configuration defined by the cubes and their intervals
The eight boxes making up *Untitled* (1967)	The "content" of this work is a negation of the assumptions one uses in formalist esthetics; Judd forces us to see a "specific" set of objects free of allusions to outside content or relational theories of composition

32. Donald Judd, Untitled, *1967. Cold-rolled steel with auto lacquer, eight boxes, each 48 x 48 x 48". Collection, Philip Johnson. Photograph courtesy Leo Castelli Gallery, New York. Photograph, Rudolph Burckhardt.*

It is important to note that the best minimalists of the 1960's usually titled their works *"Untitled."* Here is a deliberate effort to free the object of all outside traces of meaning. Like Carl Andre's, Judd's works are forerunners of Conceptualism; they need not be made by the artist, and they can function esthetically as a set of plans shown in a gallery. Again, Judd's boxes show the AIR and EARTH consistency of paintings by Stella and Albers, not overlooking their affinities to values expressed by Pollock. On the level of deliberate materiality, the issues refocus on the consistency and natural order of the materials themselves; Judd has not quite arrived at this point since he raises the issues of set theory and seriality.

Discussing Frank Stella's painting, Judd writes, "The order is not rationalistic and underlying but is simply order, like that of continuity, one thing after another" (Judd, p. 15). Short of revealing the totemistic origins of art, Judd's statements refer to it on the basic level of number and sequence. Because of the particular wholistic and materialistic quality of his esthetic, he insists that "order" and "structure" have an invented and imposed consistency in Western esthetics and rationalistic philosophy. He observes that "Obviously the means and structure couldn't be separate and couldn't even be thought of as two things joined. Neither would mean anything" (Judd, p. 15). In other words, Judd is insisting upon the inherent organic (linguistic) consistency of artistic propositions where one segregates the aspects of propositions only at the risk of destroying their internal consistency. Even as we deprive ourselves of the illusions of imposing "form," "structure," and "making" on art ideology, says Judd, we still end up with art. As we have seen, this is so for only relatively limited areas of the semiotic matrix.

33. DAN FLAVIN: THE NOMINAL THREE (TO WILLIAM OF OCKHAM) (1963–64)

Structurally Dan Flavin's art draws near to that of Judd and Carl Andre—with one important exception. Some of Flavin's early arrangements in light involved only a single fluorescent fixture. Consequently the seriality of Andre's floor constructions and the Gestalt reductivism of Judd's boxes do not play a part in Flavin's esthetic, here at least. Oddly enough these fixtures, placed in an art context, function as pure ready-mades, a fact that Duchamp might very well have recognized. With his first eight-foot strip, *the diagonal of May 25, 1963,* Flavin declared that "it seemed to sustain itself directly." These mass-produced items need not borrow from the other semiotic elements since they are the quintessential element, light itself.

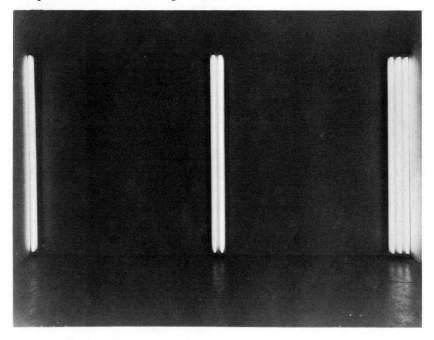

33. Dan Flavin, the nominal three (to William of Ockham), *1963/64. Cool-white fluorescent light, 8′ x 22′ x 4″. Photograph courtesy Dwan Gallery, New York.*

In his arrangement, *the nominal three,* the artist has spaced standard 8-foot fluorescent fixtures on a 22-foot wall so that the middle group is centered precisely between the two adjoining walls; the two outer groups of one and three fixtures each are butted into the corners against the walls. Again, the fixtures serve as connected subsets that function as a whole composition—as do the series of Judd's boxes. As a result EARTH is present and AIR is absent.

1. a. The arrangement as a unity   b. The arrangement *the nominal three*   c. The arrangement as six 8-foot fixtures

and

2. a. Direct illumination from the tube of every fixture   b. The illumination from *the nominal three*   c. The reflected illumination from the wall space surrounding each fixture

It is obvious why Flavin's arrangements are usually more successful than the majority of attempts in the 1960's to use light for art purposes. Most Light Art simply extends the formal vocabulary by adding new colors, degrees of brightness, or a temporal dimension to existing sculptural ideas or environments. Flavin wisely eliminates time sequences, since these destroy mythical time. He is also careful to choose only standard fixtures and standard fluorescent colors. It is also important that Flavin has insisted on noiseless, motionless environments for his arrangements. As is true of all art, he realizes that these extraneous elements destroy the mediating synthesis in his art.

In some instances, Flavin's arrangements function simultaneously as commentary on painting, sculpture, and environmentalism—yet without being specifically any one of these.

34. CARL ANDRE: The Spill (Scatter Piece) (1966)

NATURAL	CULTURAL
Andre spills several hundred small plastic blocks onto the floor from a bag (Real System A)	Basically these plastic tiles are minimal objects, rectangular forms that easily comprise eidetic images
Andre spills several hundred small plastic blocks onto the floor from a bag (Real System B)	Andre's work is composed of three connected subsets: the blocks themselves, the blocks in a bag, and the blocks on the floor
The bag and plastic blocks of *The Spill*	The "content" of this work revolves around the conceptual juxtaposition of spaces, containers, groups of materials, and the relations of the most basic objects to one another

34. Carl Andre, The Spill (Scatter Piece), *1966. Plastic blocks and canvas bag. Collection, Kimiko and John Powers, Aspen, Colorado. Photograph courtesy Dwan Gallery, New York.*

Like a number of the contemporary works mentioned previously, Carl Andre's constructions are based upon relations between the unit and the set. However it is always necessary for the set to have at least two parameters, or means of organizing the units involved. Besides the inherent order of the units, the artist depends upon room size, weight, or thermal conductivity to define the *function* of units as a whole. In Andre's words: "But my things are conceived in the world. For me, they begin in the world and the world is full of different kinds of spaces, different generic classes of spaces; inside gallery spaces, inside private dwelling spaces, inside museum spaces, inside large public spaces, and outside spaces of various kinds too. There's always a location in mind, not necessarily a specific one, but, rather, a location in scale" (Tuchman, *Artforum,* June 1970, p. 55).

Duchamp, of course, was fully aware of the mathematics controlling art like Andre's. This is brought out in his *Green Box* note of September 1915 entitled *Rattle:* "With a kind of comb, by using the space between 2 teeth as a unit, determine the relations between the 2 ends of the comb and some intermediary points (by the broken teeth)." (Duchamp, Hamilton and Hamilton.) Using the semiotics of EARTH, Duchamp is insisting that there must be two units of length defining the comb, the teeth and the spaces between them. He then describes how the comb could be used to define an ordered field of lead wires (as Duchamp used in the Chocolate Grinder). The planes generated resemble the lined configurations within some of Bridget Riley's paintings. The set relationships are the important factor.

Andre produced *Reef* in 1969 for the Whitney Museum's *Anti-Illusion: Procedures/Materials* exhibition. This work consisted of sixty-five standard styrofoam planks (these were orange since Andre wanted to avoid their looking like sculpted artifacts such as marble) wedged together in a row between two interior walls. Here the set was completed by the series of planks *and* the architectural context. The artist's plate metal "rugs" do not always succeed. Sometimes these have but one parameter, simply depending upon units of material placed in a given sequence.

35. ROBERT MORRIS: Untitled (1970) (Timbers, Concrete, and Steel Rollers)

NATURAL	CULTURAL
Under Morris's supervision the materials are hoisted into the third-floor gallery of the Whitney Museum; a double track of timber is laid along the length of the gallery; concrete blocks with rollers under them are placed over the centers of alternate ties; the ties act as fulcrums over the moving weights (Real System A)	The forms used by Morris are basic Gestalt shapes; however, once the forms have been unbalanced and made to fall in their present positions, the assembly of structural materials becomes a random "object"
The sequence of making activities as described above (Real System B)	Connected subsets are present in this construction also: the first subset is the bed of one-foot square timbers, the second is the hollow concrete blocks, and the third is formed by the rollers and gravity which allow motion between the other two components
The construction *Untitled* (1970)	*The "content" of this piece is the viewer's mental recapitulation of the making process and its implications; with a succession of slight pushes the tracks become levers, toppling the concrete blocks between the tracks; the entire process from beginning to end is viewed by spectators; various phases of it are tape-recorded and filmed*

35. *Robert Morris,* Untitled, *1970.
Timbers, concrete, steel, 7′ x 16′ x
95′. Courtesy of the artist. Photograph
courtesy Leo Castelli Gallery, New
York. Photograph, Peter Moore.*

In its last stages nonobjective art loses virtually all its abstract quality.
In a sense *Untitled* (1970) recapitulates the same use of materials and
gravity that identifies Pollock's drip paintings. When an *object,* resulting
from the making act, becomes the sole signifying convention of the art,
the semiotic of AIR has been reduced to its most fundamental level. Here
the essentials have been stressed by monumentality and costly materials;
also the making activity has been completely filmed and documented. It
is as if Morris were either attempting to understand the particular efficacy
of Pollock's painting or trying to completely transgress its principles.
Morris comes close to realizing that the making of art in terms of duration and its "esthetic" are essentially linked: "Here is the issue stated
so long ago by Duchamp: art making has to be based on other terms
than those of arbitrary, formalistic, tasteful arrangements of static forms"
(Morris, *Artforum,* April 1970, p. 65). Duchamp, of course, understood
this only too well. On another level Morris is quite aware that his work
involves the greatest departure possible from art's normal paradigmatic
plane.

It might be said that the current art with which I am dealing presents the least amount of formalistic order with an even greater order of the making behavior being implied. *It is as though the artist wants to do the most discontinuous, irrational things in the most reasonable way.* And there seems to be almost an inverse ratio at work in this progress toward the recovery of means: ever more disjunctive art acts carry even more ordered information regarding the systematic means of production. This information is increasingly allowed into the work as part of the image (Morris, *Artforum,* April 1970, p. 65, italics added).

The implications of Morris's statement are obvious: once artists begin substituting cultural objects and systems for formal relationships, nonobjective art becomes the persistent absurdity of appropriating any basic material for the process of "art making"—by this route nothing is ever represented except the will and the act behind the art itself. Beyond this there is no next step, except for the possibility of working in the environment with natural materials and systems which are, inherently, illusion free.

Since eidetic "wholeness" is the rationale behind Object Art, Minimalism underwent a steady escalation of practices during the early and middle 1960's. For instance Morris's early gray constructions were fabricated by hand with plywood; but as other artists began to use more sophisticated manufacturing techniques, resorting frequently to commercial fabrications, the need to maintain a corresponding level of standardization grew. Hand traces on these early works might subsequently be considered "esthetic articulations," thus defeating the Gestalt simplicity of Minimalism. One of Morris's most famous early pieces, his gray cornerpiece, *Untitled* (1964), fits again into the double structure of AIR and EARTH. This four-sided figure fits into the corner of any room so that only a single, equilateral triangular side is revealed to the viewer. Its double structure takes this form:

	EMPIRICAL		ESTHETIC
	$\dfrac{\text{Immediate and concrete apprehension of a form}}{\text{The triangular object}}$	$\rightleftharpoons$	$\dfrac{\text{A mental concept of a basic Gestalt image}}{\text{A simple form fabricated by the most direct means}}$
and:	$\dfrac{\text{Immediate and concrete apprehension of a form}}{\text{The triangular object}}$	$\rightleftharpoons$	$\dfrac{\text{A three-dimensional object which appears to be a two-dimensional plane}}{\text{A simple form fabricated by the most direct means}}$

The second part of the second equation above contains the logical relations of EARTH. The interconnected subsets are a triangular object, a triangular plane, connected by their context—the corner of a room. Morris's cornerpiece yields the same structure as many basic optical illusions, except in this case the illusion is partly conceptual.

Earthwork (1968) uses much the same structure, but different materials. It consisted of a pile of clean topsoil piled on a gallery carpet. Placed in the earth were a series of industrial products: heavy-duty felt stripping, lubrication grease, tubing, copper wire, steel rods, etc. In this instance industrial materials are to the "clean" earth as the "clean" earth pile is to the gallery floor (EARTH), while the assembly itself is strictly a process work (AIR).

36. RICHARD SERRA: ONE TON PROP (House of Cards) (1969)

NATURAL	CULTURAL
Four 48″ x 55″ lead plates (about 500 pounds each) which can be positioned by several people (Real System A)	Serra's arrangement simply consists of materials; these materials are not specifically connected to any Gestalt arrangement
Serra and his associates compose lead plates so that they stand on edge; each leans slightly inward, butted against the two adjacent to it in a roughly square arrangement (Real System B)	Three connected subsets composing a set are present in this piece: the floor supporting the plates, the four lead plates themselves, and gravity producing a series of compressive forces pushing inward supporting the plates each against the others
Propped lead plates	*By using unjoined parts or simple serial processes of fabrication, Serra invites mental decomposition by the viewer, stressing the fact, as Pollock did, that separations between conception and making are illusionary*

36. Richard Serra, One Ton Prop (House of Cards), *1969. Lead, 48 x 55 x 55″. Collection, George H. Waterman, III. Photograph courtesy Leo Castelli Gallery, New York. Photograph, Peter Moore.*

Among artists presently involved in process, Richard Serra best articulates the esthetic. Fundamentally this implies a fixation upon routines established by Jackson Pollock. At its most elemental level, the artist has the task of imposing the effects of gravity upon his materials so that the resulting arrangements fall into place of their own accord. In Pollock's painting gravity acts between the support and the fluid paint splashed on it; gravity defines the slope or motion, if any, accorded the canvas and the consistency of the paint. Thus the structure of EARTH gives substance to AIR.

36A. CASTING (1969)

NATURAL	CULTURAL
Molten lead splattered against the corner joint between a wall and a floor; after hardening, each casting is pulled away from the wall and a series is made (Real System A)	The castings are simply material objects, rough slabs of lead with no relevant optical properties
The same as above (Real System B)	Four connected subsets are present: molten lead, the corner itself, the forces of gravity, and the final series of castings

As a rule Process Art involves fairly simple fabrication techniques that can be reconstructed by the viewer. Formally such art has no visual meaning; its shape alone signifies nothing, while relationships between the materials and making process are critically important. Everything points to alterations made in standard materials; in Serra's case this includes arranging, splattering, fracturing, tearing, and other physical evidences of work done upon the materials.

37. HANS HAACKE: Chickens Hatching (1969)

NATURAL	CULTURAL
Eggs, eight incubators, and a brooder (Real System A)	Haacke decides to present the process of eggs hatching and the growth of baby chicks
Haacke places the above system in a museum	Logically this art work is based purely on the choice of the system by the artist
The incubator system (Real System B)	The natural process of chickens hatching
Growth of the chicks	Division of the brooder into different growth stages

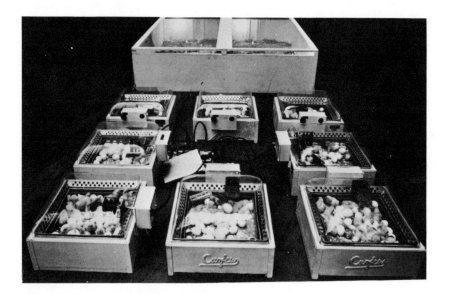

37. Hans Haacke, Chickens Hatching, *Art Gallery of Ontario, Toronto, September–October, 1969. Eight incubators, cage, chicks. Courtesy of the artist. Photograph, Hans Haacke.*

Much of Hans Haacke's work of the past six or seven years assumes the conceptual appearance of a ready-made; the artist *selects* a natural system supported by man-made equipment, allowing it to function normally in a gallery or museum environment. While such a work differs from a ready-made in that it has the appearance of FIRE, this double structure has a very particular order. Instead of the art needing two stages of preparation by the artist, the second stage in Haacke's work (as with many other artists concerned with ecological processes) is the result of change stemming from natural processes or growth patterns. Since the mythic structure of art does not provide for change or variation as a permanent feature of any work of art, the artist is either compelled to make his art finite in duration or to rely upon processes which are fundamentally *cyclical*. In *Chickens Hatching* Haacke divides the brooder into four age groups, in effect stabilizing the differences in the ages of the chickens passing through the system; but more important perhaps is the chickens' natural life-and-death cycle.

37A. SPRAY OF ITHACA FALLS: FREEZING AND MELTING ON ROPE (February 6, 7, 8 . . , 1969)

NATURAL	CULTURAL
The spray of Ithaca Falls in mid-winter; rope and screen (Real System A)	Haacke decides to suspend a rope with screening wrapped around it across Ithaca Falls
Haacke suspends the rope with the screening	A device that collects spray and ice
Rope and Screen construction (Real System B)	Weather during the 6th, 7th, and 8th of February in Ithaca
Spray and precipitation collecting on the rope and screen	A construction across the Ithaca Falls that appears to be both natural and man-made

38. DENNIS OPPENHEIM: Maze (Whitewater, Wisconsin) (1970)

NATURAL	CULTURAL
A maze diagram, cattle, and a pasture (Real System A)	From a psychology textbook the artist chooses a standard maze pattern to be built on the cow pasture
Oppenheim and his assistants construct the maze on 20,000 square feet of ground with bales of hay; cattle food is distributed at one end and the cows are led to the other end.	The cow pasture becomes in effect the maze
The cow pasture maze with cattle set at one end and food at the other (Real System B)	The instinct of cattle to find food and their intelligence in doing so
The cattle find food	By finding food the cattle demonstrate their ability to solve the maze problem

38. Dennis Oppenheim, Maze *(White-water, Wisconsin), 1970. Detail, cows at food source. Courtesy of the artist.*

Dennis Oppenheim, like Haacke, resorts to a higher structural level of FIRE. Since all art eventually divides into two activities—cognition and action—the trajectory of Oppenheim's varied interests keeps the two together on the broadest levels. In a post-painting and post-sculpture art world where end-game strategies are not entirely rewarding, this is absolutely necessary. In the artist's earlier decomposition pieces, the transplants and removals, the time and border works, the energy-material transfer projects, and the recent body works, Oppenheim continually shifts the context of his activities; yet the concern with homologies between man's activities and their effect upon the environment remains constant.

38A. ARM AND WIRE (1969)

NATURAL	CULTURAL
Arm, knotted rope, wire and nails (Real System A)	In a short black and white movie the artist documents the act of rolling his arm over a knotted rope and wire held in place by nails
The act of rolling the arm over the above materials	Here the "tool" in the form of the rope and wire leaves vivid impressions on the arm which is the power source of the act
Impressions in the skin of the arm (Real System B)	The natural metabolic functions of the human body
Gradual fading of the wire and rope impressions from the skin of the arm	The fact that the skin on the arm returns to its normal texture and color is the cyclical inversion in this form of Body Art

39. LES LEVINE: Systems Burn-off X Residual Software (1969)

NATURAL	CULTURAL
Critics and artists attending the press preview of the Cornell University Earth Art Exhibition (Real System A)	Levine decides to photograph artists and critics attending the press preview of the Cornell Earth Art Exhibition
Levine photographs the artists and critics; he selects 31 photographs and has these reproduced to offset on typewriter paper 1000 times each	Artists and critics, *not* the Earth Art Exhibition itself, are the subject of Levine's work; professional responses to an art exhibition become a source of art
31,000 photographs of artists and critics looking at the Earth Art Exhibition (Real System B)	Levine decides to show the Earth Art Exhibition photographs scattered on the floor of a gallery
A third of the photographs are randomly distributed by Levine's assistant on the floor of the gallery; the results are covered with liquid raspberry Jell-O; single copies are affixed to the walls of the gallery with chewing gum	Levine insists that the work has nothing to do with Abstract Expressionism since he has had no personal involvement in the making process; he is implicitly stating that all avant-garde art stems from the residual effects of past art

39. Les Levine, Systems Burn-off X Residual Software, *1969. Courtesy of the artist.*

Les Levine's art is historically transgressive and therefore unpredictable. Occasionally the artist produces something which appears to fit one category of making, but really belongs to another. Structurally *Systems Burn-off* resembles Duchamp's *L.H.O.O.Q.*, the Mona Lisa with a penciled-in moustache and goatee. Levine is making art from the residual effects of avant-garde art, but with several modifications. On one level *Systems Burn-off* is a somewhat conventional elaboration of abstract expressionist techniques. On another level it implies that the Earth Art exhibition at Cornell was in no way avant-garde or antiart, but merely an extension of Formalism supported by the media. In other words, the works created are temporary; only media records are historical. The strewn photographs alternately become trash or expressionistic gestures after being covered with raspberry Jell-O. This naturalizes what is essentially a series of cultural acts.

Recently Levine proposed a process piece in Canada which was so costly and complicated that it could not be completed by those assigned to do it. Here the idea of conceptual recapitulation is completely frustrated. The particular direction taken by Levine is one recognizing that Formalism and its limits are already dead ends, leaving the artist with very little if any mobility. Note Levine's statement: "What I'm trying to point out is that art is a locked-in system at this stage, so much so that it doesn't need to be done because all locked-in systems prechoice themselves. From now on you don't have to make art because art will make itself."

40. DOUGLAS HUEBLER: Duration Piece No. 15—Global (September, 1969)

NATURAL	CULTURAL
The fugitive Edmund Kite McIntyre as specified in an F.B.I. "Wanted" poster (Real System A)	Artist's statement: "Beginning on January 1, 1970 a reward of $1,100.00 will be paid to the person who provides the information resulting in the arrest and conviction of Edmund Kite McIntyre wanted by the Federal Bureau of Investigation for Bank Robbery (Title 18, U. S. Code, Section 2113a and 2113d). On February 1, 1970 $100.00 will be reduced from that first offer making it $1,000.00; it will be reduced another $100.00 on the first day of each subsequent month until there will exist no reward at all on January 1, 1971." Huebler further states that the owner will be responsible for the reward in case the piece is purchased before 1971
Huebler furnishes the poster and the statement of his obligations as the completed piece—except for any ensuing documents pertaining to the capture and conviction of the suspect	McIntyre is not convicted and/or no one collects the reward established by the artist for the 1970 year period
Same as the signifier for the Plane of Content above (Real System B)	Same as the signified for the Plane of Content above
Huebler furnishes documents and pays the reward	McIntyre is captured and convicted and the party responsible collects the reward

40. *Douglas Huebler,* Duration Piece
No. 15—Global, *1969. Courtesy of
the artist.*

Douglas Huebler's works are unusual for Conceptual Art because the
artist wants to retain the usual artistic involvement of both decision and
fabrication. Frequently his ideas include time continua through past, present, and future; also it is not unusual for Huebler to involve the viewer
or buyer directly in the making experience. *Duration Piece No. 15* has no
meaning in terms of visual values; it is, in fact, a constructed set of relationships, nothing more. Structurally Huebler is equating the "capturing" of art (through buying) with the capturing of a known criminal. In
both instances what is sought is fugitive and its value is shifting. While the
owner is made personally aware of the transaction, the artist increment-
ally expurgates his own involvement by using the profit from selling the
art to pay for the reward. Thus as a form of social exchange, the piece
balances.

Many of Huebler's conceptual works involve the element FIRE since a future possibility or choice results in more than one kernel structure. Others, such as *Location Piece No. 23—Los Angeles–Cape Cod* (August, 1969), pertain to EARTH. Using a beach near his cottage at Truro, Massachusetts, Huebler decides to use the dimensions of a gallery in Los Angeles as boundaries for six sites on the beach. Markers are placed at the six locations and Huebler makes photographs of each. These are assembled with a map and explanation and the piece is sent to the gallery in Los Angeles. The result on the gallery goer's part is a sense of double transposition.

a. The gallery in Los Angeles

b. The photos of the Truro beach with the gallery floor markers

c. The sites on Truro beach with markers the dimensions of the gallery floor

41. BERNAR VENET: The Logic of Decision and Action (Photograph) (1969)

NATURAL	CULTURAL
A recent text entitled *The Logic of Decision and Action*—as opposed to all past decisions and activities concerned with intuitive art making, specifically all formal problems such as form, color, composition, materials, space and so on	Venet decides to select a given "domain" because of its importance to society, thus the artist strives for the presentation of "objective knowledge"
The title and table of contents of this book are photographed, enlarged, and mounted for display	*The Logic of Decision and Action* is an analysis of linguistical structure; therefore it is also a tract on esthetics
A photographic enlargement of *The Logic of Decision and Action*	The "content" of this display is the logical bind between the concept of historical progress through the evolution of knowledge structures and the historical concept of art itself
Venet's manifesto of 1967 and subsequent writings by him	This is a form of quasi-Conceptualism which threatens to unseat art by the types of information chosen as subject matter

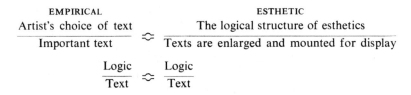

41. *Bernar Venet,* The Logic of Decision and Action, *1969. Photograph,
60 x 80". Courtesy of the artist.*

Bernar Venet is implying that new-knowledge syntheses are a normal
aspect of human cultural development and therefore "natural." His choice
of the book *The Logic of Decision and Action* has a two-edged implication: for one, he is presenting a text which to some extent reveals the constancy of the structure of art-making; at the same time through the dialectical, and thus historical, progression of knowledge as an integral aspect of the human condition, he is subverting the historical-mythic structure behind all avant-garde art. Like Daniel Buren, Venet presents post-
Duchampian art which questions present epistomological assumptions in
as exacting a way.

$$\frac{\text{EMPIRICAL}}{\text{Artist's choice of text}} \underset{\backsim}{\frown} \frac{\text{ESTHETIC}}{\text{The logical structure of esthetics}}$$
$$\frac{\text{Important text}}{} \qquad \frac{\text{Texts are enlarged and mounted for display}}{}$$

$$\frac{\text{Logic}}{\text{Text}} \underset{\backsim}{\frown} \frac{\text{Logic}}{\text{Text}}$$

42. JOSEPH KOSUTH: SYNOPSIS OF CATEGORIES (1968)

The Linguistic Conceptualism of Joseph Kosuth is an attempt to investigate the logic of art as it parallels language. Kosuth reveals aspects of the conceptual organization of art by framing art propositions which in themselves mirror art as a system of social usage. In the *Synopsis of Categories* the artist defines a group of classifications and then divides each of these into sections. Under the sections he lists a series of terms chosen from a thesaurus; both synonyms and antonyms are included from the terms given in a standard thesaurus. Structurally, the *Synopsis* is defined by four *interconnected* subsets through the semiotic of EARTH.

a. The classes of terms

b. Topics under classes

c. Individual word entries

d. The Synopsis itself

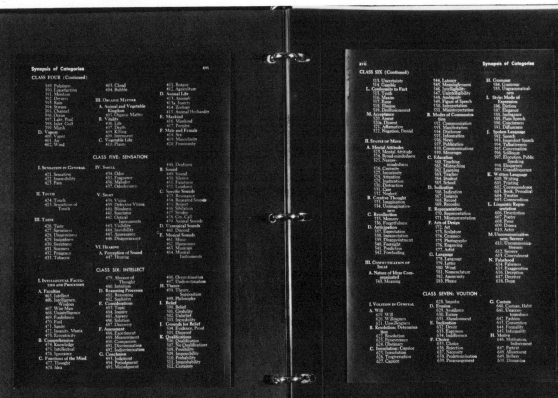

42. *Joseph Kosuth,* Synopsis of Categories, *1968. Courtesy of the artist. Photograph courtesy Leo Castelli Gallery, New York. Photograph, Pollitzer.*

Joseph Kosuth's work as an art investigator (artist) has steadily sharpened in focus since his first definition in 1965, *One of Three Chairs*. Again, this piece (consisting of a wooden folding chair, an enlarged photograph of the chair, and a dictionary definition of a chair) operates as three interconnected subsets. Kosuth in his writings reminds us that fifty years ago philosophy passed through the stage of internal revelation which art is now entering. In applying logical and linguistical concepts to art, Kosuth insists, and rightly so, that art is an analytic system whose validity "depends solely on the definitions of the symbols it contains (according to the philosopher A. J. Ayer)." In effect he is saying that art is a form of logic which allows for the substitution of a group of objects, an identity, or an idea as terms in a proposition, so long as the syntactical rules of the system are observed. It follows that this book is an attempt to define some of those rules and to provide explanations for their presence. Kosuth maintains that as long as art is discussed in terms of art ideas, the results will be an exchange of tautologies. Only by revealing the structural relationships between ideas can we transcend art on the ideological level, as did some aspects of philosophy after 1914.

Works such as the *Synopsis of Categories* are frequently resented within the art world because Kosuth chooses words instead of pictorial images to represent signs. In essence, the artist is implying that art is a system of signs which demands more and more obvious components to meet the tendency toward greater simplification.

Mel Ramsden of The Society of Theoretical Art and Analysis produced a thesaurus work similar but not identical to Kosuth's. This set of thesaurus categories entitled *Six Negatives* is explained as follows:

> The synopsis of categories was used in "Six Negatives" partly in the sense of a ready-made. The synopsis acts not specifically as an object (in the current usage) but rather an indication or "picture" of a totality of our language and ideas, a "world view." The selection of this was to be able to indicate the presence of this totality as a system within the work, the idea of the Thesaurus per se partially forming the idea of the work. After the synopsis has been altered through the "negations," the "picture of the world view" is no longer viable, while still acting as a reference it misrepresents. As such, the synopsis indicates the system from which it derives, but only as a *representation* since it must exclude the system "as a whole." The identification of the whole system with the new context would imply the inclusion of the meaning and the sense of the system (and thus its functioning as part of the Thesaurus),

then the art condition would be the actual synopsis in every sense so it could no longer logically be an art condition. (Ian Burn, *Conceptual Art and Conceptual Aspects,* p. 23.)

With the negation of representational features and formal relations as the essence of the modernist syndrome, it would seem that Ramsden is, like Kosuth, supplying words instead of pictorial elements for sign. *Six Negatives* is not a pure ready-made (AETHER); rather it resembles a semi-ready-made. Ramsden's subtractions in a sense help to define the work just as much as the words he has left. Since the work contains "content,' its structure most approximates EARTH.

1. The set of classes (at least three)
2. The set of subtopics within the classes
3. The set of items within each subtopic

43. DANIEL BUREN: Photographic Souvenir of One of the Pieces Executed in Kyoto, Japan (1970)

NATURAL	CULTURAL
All works are on printed paper with 3⅜ inch-wide vertical stripes, alternating white with a color chosen by the artist; these may be affixed to any surface, interior or exterior	The system has visual meaning only on the most elementary level of Gestalt perception
The system of striped paper in a specified location	*Buren is adamant in his insistence that his system has no "content," either visually or on a metalanguage level*
Buren's writing about his own work and the art of other artists; Michel Claura's writing about Buren	Buren's decision not to comment on the content or structure of his art (AIR) is in itself a metalanguage statement

43. Daniel Buren, Photographic Souvenir of One of the Pieces Executed in Kyoto, Japan, *1970. Courtesy of the artist. Photograph, Hans Haacke.*

Daniel Buren's work may be repeated *ad infinitum* with no formal evolution or illusionistic implications. Buren has read Lévi-Strauss and Barthes well since he understands that terms in a natural series, or signifiers, must be opposed or they remain nonart. Nevertheless he insists that his art remains "unframed" while all art in the context of history is "framed." But in fact the "frame" or cultural term opposing his work is the historical formal category. This is true also of some recent Conceptual Art, where an "object" is created in terms of latent art intuition. As Barthes claims, the absence of any specific signified in language transforms a signifier into a signified on another plane; this is "zero degree" art where power is given to a system of signs to create meaning out of nothing.

Buren's article "Beware!" (*Studio International,* March, 1970, pp. 100–04) is probably the most succinct statement yet to appear on painting and the art historical crisis. In a most elegant, but not theoretically revealing way, the author touches upon the issues of illusionism, repetition (commercial, esthetic, and hypnotic), anonymity (and its counterparts), and viewpoint or context as it affects art propositions. The larger implication of Buren's work is his recognition of its destructive potential as a political proposition with far-reaching implications. He writes: "It may be affirmed that all art up to the present day has been created on the one hand only *empirically* and on the other out of idealistic thinking. If it is possible to think again or to think and create theoretically/scientifically, the *rupture* will be achieved and thus the work of art will have lost the meanings—numerous and divergent—which at present encumber it. We can say, on the basis of the foregoing, that the rupture, if any, can be (can only be) epistemological. This rupture is/will be the resulting logic of a theoretical work at the moment when the history of art (which is still to be made) and its application are/will be envisaged theoretically; theory and theory alone, as we well know, can make possible a revolutionary practice. Furthermore, not only is/will theory be indissociable from its own practice, but again it may/will be able to give rise to other original kinds of practice."

Buren ends this statement with: "We are aware that this exposition of facts may be somewhat didactic; nevertheless we consider it indispensable to proceed in this way at this time" (Buren, *S.I.,* p. 104).

IV

Marcel Duchamp: *MAGISTER LUDI*

The artist I believe in;
the art is a mirage.

—Marcel Duchamp
from a television program taped in 1964

We might begin by asking why Marcel Duchamp went to the trouble of writing a book on a very rare situation in chess. The book, entitled *L'Opposition et les Cases conjuguées sont réconciliées* (1932), treats the moves in end-game play when both Kings are left alone on the board, with only a few blocked pawns. Such a predicament demands that both Kings play very cautiously, avoiding certain squares at all cost, but at the same time moving in synchronization across the board totally (or seemingly) oblivious to each other. The authors of this treatise, Duchamp and Vitaly Halberstadt, were the first to have recognized that these movements (Zugzwang) are logically related to each other. One reviewer of their book notes that the authors have extended the idea of *opposition* in chess to the contrasting concepts of *orthodox opposition* and *heterodox opposition*. Heterodox opposition, he insists, is just an amplification of the techniques used in orthodox opposition. But the use of methods which extend beyond and transgress ordinary opposition is also implied. Could it be that Duchamp was actually mapping out the strategies which any artist would have to use in end-game play in art?

It is evident from the previous chapter that, as the usable terms of art diminish, terms which complete oppositions became increasingly unorthodox. We should comment on two other factors. Arturo Schwarz translates the chess book title as *Opposition and Sister Squares Are Reconciled* (Schwarz, p. 62); this relates to the principle of *double opposition* which dominates the semiotic relationships controlling art and language, i.e., the four-part matrix of the real system and the FIRE–AIR and WATER–EARTH relationships defining basic types of art. For the cover of the book, Duchamp photographed an image of the title made by exposing stenciled letters to the sun. And in fact the sun and the color yellow retain a central

158

significance in the creation of *The Large Glass*. In January 1914, Duchamp produced a curious drawing of a figure hunched over the handlebars of a bicycle, pedaling uphill with great exertion into the sun, entitled *To Have the Apprentice in the Sun*. As a preliminary note for *The Large Glass*, some critics feel that the drawing depicts Duchamp; but while it may, it also represents the plight of any artist striving for artistic insight through his own work. Perhaps it is only Duchamp who was not blinded by the sun, a symbol of revelation.

Where Duchamp would observe that "all chess players are artists," he might also insist that all linguists are closer to the mechanisms of art. Robert Lebel notes that as early as 1911 Duchamp and Picabia had gained various insights into word play and its conceptual importance to art, through a performance of Raymond Roussel's *Impressions d'Afrique* (Lebel, p. 7). From Schwarz's writing, it seems likely that Duchamp, by 1912 or 1913, had grasped the essential relationships between language as an evolving set of positional signs, and art as its semiotic, but perhaps simpler, counterpart (Schwarz, "A New Society and a New Language," pp. 28–30). In fact, Schwarz relates Duchamp's desire "to transfer the significance of language from words into signs, into a visual expression of the word, similar to the ideogram of the Chinese language" (Schwarz, p. 29). In some detail the author discloses how this metaphorical expression of signs relates to the mystery of *The Large Glass*. The "new" grammatical relations which Duchamp sought are in part phonetically derived. Duchamp indicates that "If what you want is a grammatical rule: the verb agrees with the subject in consonance; for instance, *le nègre aigrit, les négresses s'aigrissent ou maigrissent,* etc." (Schwarz, p. 30). Here, of course, is Roland Barthes's observation that most creativity results from extending the terms of a system onto the syntagmatic plane so that they become linguistically united. Some time before the publication of these puns the artist shifted phonetic displacements to the sphere of objects and their contexts. The *Bottle Rack* (1914) becomes a matter of altering or destroying systematic relationships, that is, of removing the utensil from a kitchen and placing it in an art gallery. (In a less informed way, from 1911 Picasso and Braque did the same thing with collage materials.) Thus it seems that Duchamp's observation, "There is no solution because there is no problem," is born of an understanding that art is a fragile system of signs and values, where each "solution" is in fact a step toward eliminating the chance of subsequent solutions. There is no such thing as an "art problem" because art as a self-conscious system devolves merely by existing in a problematic form. Art's instability is a death wish, as Duchamp indicated many times. In a footnote on ready-mades, Schwarz quotes from a dialogue between Lévi-Strauss and Georges Charbonnier, in which the former says, "I think we are on the borders of a confusion that would be extremely dangerous. It is not each object in itself that is a work of art, it is particular arrangements, dispositions of objects, particular relationships among objects that result in a work of art. Just like the words of a language, for example. Taken alone, words are weak in, almost void of meaning. They only really take on a meaning in context" (Schwarz, p. 38).

In terms of what we know about Duchamp's command over the subtleties of language—through puns and titles—can this tell us anything about *The Large Glass?* Schwarz observes that the title, *La Mariée mise à nu par ses célibataires, même* could be pronounced so that *même* becomes *m'aime,* or *The Bride stripped bare by her bachelors is in love with me* (Schwarz, p. 79). Quite simply Duchamp is relating that many artists may try to win or cultivate art, but Duchamp already has her. Octavio Paz mentions that the use of the term *célibataire* does not imply suitor or fiancé, but rather a number of men—bachelors—whose position as far as marriage is concerned seems to be rather negative. The term *mise à nu,* he insists, is not related to love but to something much more brutal, a public stripping (Paz). Thus what Duchamp implies is that although artists will in time strip art of her signifying power, Duchamp has done it already—leaving a Bride who is not virgin.

In his notes for *The Green Box,* the artist refers to *The Large Glass* as "a world in yellow." Schwarz catches the revelationary and ambivalent qualities of the word, as well as its significance as a symbol for Eros. In a larger sense it stands for the creative force itself.

EROS = Art = Language

Yellow, moreover, is a sign of hope; as Lüscher indicates in his personality test through color: "If yellow is chosen in 1st place, it shows the desire for release and the hope or expectation of greater happiness, and implies some minor or major conflict from which release was needed. This hope of happiness, in all of its countless forms from sexual adventure to philosophies offering enlightenment and perfection, is always directed towards the future; yellow presses forward, towards the new, the modern, the developing and the unformed" (Lüscher, p. 63). The *Glass,* of course, represents Duchamp's victory over art and at the same time, frees him from the obligation to create art. Robert Lebel looks upon the *Glass* as a kind of catharsis, one that helped to release the artist from earlier neuroses. The *Glass* liberates Duchamp because symbolically it foretells the evolutionary pattern of future art. In a similar sense Duchamp's subtitle, *Delay in Glass,* refers to nothing visual, but rather to the fact that completion of *The Large Glass* is a matter of waiting until it is recognized that avant-garde art is essentially a closed system. This is probably the only reason why Duchamp ceased work on the project in 1923.

Eventually a more complete analysis of Duchamp's notes for *The Green Box* will appear, since they represent the verbal counterpart to the *Glass's* iconography. But two notes in the preface are important here (Duchamp, Hamilton, and Hamilton). In the first, Duchamp seems completely aware of the possibilities—"according to certain laws"—afforded to all signifiers and signifieds. He even makes an "Algebraic comparison":

$$\frac{a}{b}$$ a being the exposition

   b " the possibilities

the ratio $\dfrac{a}{b}$ is in no way given by a

number c $\dfrac{a}{b}$ = c but by the sign $^{(-)}$ which separates

a and b; a and b being "<u>known</u>,, they become

new   relative
units and lose their numerical value   (or in duration);

                of ratio
; the sign $-\int$which separated them remains (<u>sign of the</u>

                        ?
<u>accordance</u> or rather <u>of</u> . . . . . . <u>look for it</u>)

Duchamp at this point takes pains to explain that his use of the symbol of ratio has nothing to do with division, but rather with some other shift in value. "Exposition" (*a*) refers to signifier or syntagm, while "possibilities" (*b*) refers to signified or system. So, in all probability, a *"sign of the accordance"* means the two parts function semiologically.

Following this in the Hamilton edition of *The Green Box* is an early note from 1912. In part it reads:

The machine with 5 hearts, the pure child of nickel and platinum must dominate the Jura–Paris road.

On the one hand, the chief of the 5 nudes will be ahead of the 4 other nudes towards this Jura–Paris road. On the other hand, the headlight child will be the instrument conquering this Jura–Paris road.

The "machine with 5 hearts" is the Alchemist's Stone, the Great Pyramid, or the semiotic structure including AETHER, FIRE, WATER, AIR, and EARTH. In reality the Jura-Paris road runs from the Jura Mountains at the Swiss border to Paris. Moreover, there is a Jura Mountain Range on the Moon. The Moon being a symbol of the female and natural, it seems likely that Duchamp is implying that the "evolution of art" is the traversal from the completely cultural to the totally natural. The "chief of the 5 nudes" refers to Picasso and his pivotal cubist painting of 1907, *Les Demoiselles d'Avignon*. The "headlight child," however, is Duchamp. He is stating that the path of Cubism—"retinal painting"—will seem to overshadow art, but that he and his insights will dominate art in the end.

> This headlight child could, graphically, be a comet, which would have its tail in front, this tail being an appendage of the headlight child appendage which absorbs by crushing (gold dust, graphically) this Jura–Paris road.

A comet with "its tail in front" is the trajectory of Duchamp's work between 1911 and 1926. In that short span of time he managed to anticipate in some fashion practically every art movement subsequently to arise in art history. It follows that the tail of the comet "absorbs" the content, that is, all new work, along the path of the Jura–Paris road.

> The Jura–Paris road, having to be infinite only humanly, will lose none of its character of infinity in finding a termination at one end in the chief of the five nudes, at the other in the headlight child.
> The term "indefinite" seems to me more accurate than infinite. The road will begin in the chief of the 5 nudes, and will not end in the headlight child.

The Jura–Paris road seems "infinite" only because no artist except Duchamp had the knowledge to anticipate how art would end. A more reasonable interpretation would be that Duchamp never predicted the end of art, but only the modern historical phase. Art remains a matter of devising infinite variations through commonly held sign systems. The road, nevertheless, is "indefinite" because it is a temporal pathway, not a matter of distance. While the road continues with the discoveries of Picasso, Duchamp as the "headlight child" refuses to terminate it; this he leaves to future artists. His note ends by describing painting as a semiotic system in gradual deterioration. Eventually it becomes "without topographical form" (purely conceptual) "which finds its opening towards the infinite in the headlight child." Duchamp finishes with the decision that his allegory

44. *Marcel Duchamp,* The Bride Stripped Bare by Her Bachelors, Even (The Large Glass), *1915–1923. Oil and wire on glass, 109¼″ high. Courtesy, Philadelphia Museum of Art. Louise and Walter Arensberg Collection. Photograph, A. J. Wyatt, staff photographer.*

on the evolution and finale of art will be signified by the use of wood for the Jura–Paris road, wood being the material first chosen for the surface of *The Bride Stripped Bare* (Duchamp, Hamilton, and Hamilton).

The structure of *The Large Glass* is twofold: an upper female section and a lower male section. This diptych arrangement corresponds to the $\frac{a}{b}$ or signifier-signified relationship which he proposes in the first notes in *The Green Box*. It follows that this female-male relationship is consistent with the Natural-Cultural dichotomies set up by Lévi-Strauss. In terms of style, the "exposition" or female section relates to Cubism or that mode of art activity established by "the chief of the 5 nudes," while the lower section—those "possibilities" or antisystemic devices worked out by Duchamp—are strictly derived from post-cubist activities. So in general, the upper or Bride section of the *Glass* is historically oriented, while the lower or Bachelor section is ahistorical or even antihistorical in its implications. This again reinforces the relationship of the art historian to the artist in a diachronic mythic structure: power over all ideal time as opposed to power over the moment.

Given the above clues, unraveling the iconography of *The Large Glass* is a matter of patience and scholarship. Since a full denouement of the work is not our purpose, we will touch on a few details in such a way as to make it obvious that the *Glass* is, in fact, a coherent allegory of the devolution of modern art in terms of Duchamp's own psychosexual catharsis. One wonders if Arturo Schwarz was made privy to the artist's secrets. Of all the biographers and interpreters of Duchamp, he by far gives the most tantalizing insights into the *Glass's* underlying significance.

The Bride, on the esthetic or self-referential level, is the state of art in the modern world. As Lebel indicates, "theoretically this Virgin is destined to become the Bride, for her fulfillment, Duchamp emphasizes, will cause her downfall and instead it is essential for her to preserve herself in a sort of ambiguously intermediary state" (Lebel, p. 14). "Intermediary" means that while, due to Duchamp, she is no longer a virgin, total fulfillment would simply make it impossible for her to exist at all. The Bride is "a sort of apotheosis of virginity," in other words, glorification of a previously held state. Connections between the Bride and the Bachelors through the stripping process are "electrical," thus invisible and physical. Duchamp then adds the phrase, "Short circuit if necessary," which means that he may precipitate the stripping routine through his own ready-mades and optical experiments.

He refers to the Bride as "a sort of automobiline with quite feeble cylinders" whose "desire-gears . . . are only the string that binds the bouquet." The Bride is the atrophied art impulse of the modern era, which is kept alive only by the desire to have the Bride. The Bride's "cinematic blossoming" is the future development of painting seen in retrospect—this is made rather explicit. Duchamp also describes how the Bride will reveal herself: "the first, that of the stripping by the Bachelors, the second appearance that voluntary-imaginative one of the Bride." It is evident that as artists strip art of her signifying power, art will give up or reveal her underlying logical mechanisms. The Bride is at times referred to as the "pendu femelle" or literally, hanging female element. Schwarz suggests that Duchamp has executed the Bride before she has had a chance to commit a crime. But it is also true that the hanging of paintings will in time contribute to the Bride's downfall, just as Duchamp has mercifully saved the Bride from a public execution by killing (having intercourse/ incest with) her first.

The upper portion of the Bride section of the *Glass* is filled with a grayish cloudy area alternately referred to as the "Top Inscription," "Milky Way," or the "cinematic blossoming." This area is punctuated by three squarish holes referred to as the "draft pistons," "triple cipher," or "nets." Actually these provide power for the Bride machine, while at the same time they determine the Bride's commands. In his directions for a "moving inscription" Duchamp proposes that a series of alphabetic units (perhaps A, B, C, D . . . and so on) be added and superimposed over each other one at a time as a sequence of photographic negatives. These were to be etched onto the *Glass* in the spaces provided by the "draft pistons," but this was found to be too difficult technically. (Needless to say, Jasper Johns undertook a quite similar series of number and alphabet paintings.) Duchamp realized (probably around 1913 or 1914) that iconic signs comprise a syntax which can be integrated with and superimposed upon various existing pictorial conventions. Signs, numbers, or letters work equally well in demonstrating that modernist esthetics depends upon the reduction of signifying terms. As a result these inscriptions define the state of art, and in doing so give "commands" to the Bride. Subsequently, but not finally, the inscriptions were changed to *impressions* of three gauze nets placed on the Milky Way; these screenlike imprints thus became symbols of blank canvases upon which subsequent art (past, present, and future) might be inscribed: "Next remove them so that nothing remains but their firm imprint i.e., the *form* permitting all combinations of letters sent across this said triple form, commands, orders, authorizations, etc. which must join the shots and the splash. . . ." (Duchamp, Hamilton, and Hamilton).

Occupying the middle right-hand area of the Bride section one finds the last group of elements, the Nine Shots. These are nine encircled holes (later drilled), located by having fired a toy cannon nine times at a given target point on the *Glass*. Most probably these points, a mixture of randomness and skill, represent the efforts of individual artists to penetrate the Bride. In his notes Duchamp writes: "—With maximum skill, this projection would be reduced to a point (the target). With ordinary skill this projection will be a demultiplication of the target." In effect he is saying that any artist who has a profound understanding of art may turn it into a system, while normally even the best artists simply reduce art's capacity of signification.

As creator of *The Large Glass* Duchamp maintains a peculiar and ambivalent relationship with its male and female components. At times he intimates an opposition and identity to both. For instance, Duchamp's role as Rose Sélavy (his chosen female alter-ego), and his insistence that works of art demand a balance of male-female characteristics is maintained in the description of the Top Inscription or Milky Way. In French, as Ulf Linde points out, the Milky Way *(Voie Lactée)* can also be pronounced as *voile acté,* or *acted veil.* In other words the Top Inscription is the Bride's veil but also that screen which hides the underlying meaning of every work of art from the viewer. Arturo Schwarz, commenting on the androgynous character of the Top Inscription, states that only in this area is the mixture of the Bride's Water and the Bachelors' Gas resolved and unified. Apparently the Top Inscription represents artistic synthesis.

Initially for the bottom half of the *Glass,* Duchamp had planned eight bachelors in the form of Malic Molds. Later a ninth bachelor or a stationmaster was added. One might speculate that the original forms represent the eight pawns in chess. It is also possible that the ninth represents Duchamp as "stationmaster" or guide into the future. Schwarz observes that three and multiples of three dominate the entire *Glass,* and for Duchamp three symbolizes the multitude or masses when raised to the second power, or nine. So that while Duchamp transcends the usual run of artists, he is also one of them. Furthermore, the Malic Molds were to be painted different colors. (This is in reference to Baudelaire's essay on "The Salon of 1846" where the poet observes that universal equality has produced an immense number of men who are no more than "undertaker's mutes" afflicted with the same drab, hardly varying uniforms.) But the Malic Molds were left in red lead underpaint, symbolizing perhaps the primeval color of death. Duchamp coined the word "Malic," referring to them as "malish," which in turn implies *male, metallic* and *malic acid,* as well as the German term "to paint," *malen.* Hence in Duchamp's mind the "Nine Malic Molds" represent an unfeeling or unseeing fragment of humanity posing as artists, people who wear different clothes and posture in a variety of ways. As a group—not as individuals—he obviously held his peers in low esteem. On another level he implies that most artists need a *uniform* to convince themselves of their own identity. One remembers that Duchamp spent the latter part of his life disengaging from the artist's role, but at the same time never denying his own artistry. In looking at the Malic Molds as hollow metal forms filled with "illuminating gas" from the Bride's Machine, he is reaffirming the part that the desire for fame and recognition plays in the average artist's life.

From a flow diagram of the parts of *The Large Glass* drawn by Richard Hamilton (Duchamp, Hamilton, and Hamilton), it seems reasonable that the piece not only represents a summation of Duchamp's feelings about art and life, but also the way in which ideas are transformed (or transmuted) into art. The lower half registers the complexities of art as a human psychological problem, while the upper half concerns itself with those sociopsychological phenomena that account for the fact that only *some* objects become art. Hamilton's diagram reveals that, despite several feedback loops, the general flow of the Bride's "love gasoline" is clockwise, while the direction of the Bachelors' "illuminating gas" and "spangles" is counterclockwise. Thus the area of artistic transformation, or in Duchampian nomenclature the "mirror image of splash," is situated on the right side of the *Glass*. The "mirror image" probably refers to the inversion of terms necessary to create any work of art. Here in the area of reflection and adjacent to the proposed "stripping mechanism," one finds the seemingly metaphysical means by which new works alter the art condition. These mechanisms on the right side of the *Glass* (perhaps representing the future) are the least finished. If, as appears quite likely, they also signify the depletion of art, then it follows that this acts as a "transmitter" of events which will take place sometime after Duchamp's "incompletion" of *The Large Glass*.

Both the Bride's and the Bachelors' mechanisms contain several references to Y-shaped arbors and hooks. Schwarz interprets these as symbols of bisexuality and immortality, and also as religious traditions linking the two traits. If the *Glass* actually does unlock the pattern of modern artistic creation, then identification with immortality seems well-placed (not omitting the overturned yoke of the Bicycle Wheel, and its allusion to Kharma, in the artist's first ready-made).

To the right foreground of the Malic Molds, Duchamp has placed a metal-framed structure on runners variously referred to as the "Chariot," "Sleigh," or "Glider." The Chariot moves back and forth over a very short span of track. Its "litanies" or "Exposé" are phrases such as "Slow life," "Vicious circle," "Onanism," "Cheap Construction," "Eccentrics," and "Monotonous fly wheel"—as if to say that art is invariably made in the same way with simple materials; art never "progresses" or uses anything of consequence. The "Buffer of life" or springs controlling the motion of the Chariot is explained with this note: "stopping action not by brutal opposition but by extended springs slowly resuming their first position." "Brutal opposition" would disclose the structure of art; instead Duchamp allows art to proceed on its own trajectory through the constant oscillation of different sign combinations. In part, the Chariot is controlled by the weight of "brand bottles" which may refer to works of art with titles affecting their esthetic valency (Duchamp, Hamilton, and Hamilton).

Dominating the lower center of the Bachelor Machine is the Chocolate Grinder, consisting of three rotating drums supported by a base with Louis XV legs. Accompanying this is the artist's famous epithet: "The bachelor grinds his chocolate himself—." The intentions of the Chocolate Grinder repeat the themes of onanism and narcissism found elsewhere in the Bachelor Machine. Duchamp simply implies what is already well known, namely that solitariness and self-gratification dominate the psyche of the artist; at the same time they account for the essential bachelor's role which all artists play vis-à-vis women and family. Grinding chocolate relates to the grinding of paint pigments—it must be remembered that when Duchamp traveled alone to Munich in 1912 he studied paint and painting techniques to ensure the highest quality for his last few canvases. Mounted on the Chocolate Grinder are the Bayonet and Scissors, two Freudian objects that reinforce the perpetual theme of male castration and the fears which provoke artistic creation. To the rear of these two objects is The Network of Standard Stops or "sieves." These are six conical-shaped filters which purify the "illuminating gas." Duchamp's process for making these is curious in that he coated the sieves separately and allowed dust to settle on each for a given period of time. Hence the last sieve to the right side is coated with the most dust. It seems reasonable that the sieves are only partially concerned with purification; since they imply an inversion of their usual function, it is more than likely that they represent time and its effects on the perception of art.

Situated below the blades of the Scissors are three elliptical drawings, the Oculist Witnesses. About these Arturo Schwarz comments, "In fact, the Bride needs the cooperation of the Oculist Witnesses to meet the Bachelors and thus achieve her orgasm since, as we have already seen, the Bachelors (drops) will meet her only after being dazzled across the Oculist Charts" (Schwarz, p. 181). Quite probably the Oculist Witnesses represent critics or other influential tastemakers in the art world, while the Oculist's Charts may refer to criticism and art historical documents. In the notes with the Oculist's Charts, but never included in the "unfinished"

Glass, is the Wilson-Lincoln system. This optical illusion reveals profiles of both presidents through movements of a viewer's head. The Wilson-Lincoln system is the simplest visual representation of the ability of sign signifiers to express two or more ideas conceptually.

Schwarz has stressed in his descriptions of the iconography of the *Glass* that the work is literally mythic, or in Duchamp's words, "the picture is an apparition of an appearance." It is in fact a myth about a myth. Largely the myth is concerned with the fallibility of cultures which accept their sign systems as empirical truths. But *The Large Glass* with its puns and allusions is also a most elegant attempt to create a summarizing work of art by explaining the structure of art, setting in motion the kind of dialectical or capping process by which every semiological system transcends its predecessors. Only at this stage does one begin to grasp the magnitude of restraint and psychic complexity involved in the Duchamp Myth. It seems likely that what made it possible for Duchamp to live with this secret for over fifty years was the sublime assurance that his wisdom and oracular powers would one day be appreciated far beyond what was possible in his lifetime.

Quite early, the study of literature and linguistics became central to Duchamp's development. In Arturo Schwarz's words, "On more than one occasion, while discussing the origins of the work [*The Large Glass*], Duchamp has singled out the writings of Jean-Pierre Brisset and Raymond Roussel—two writers who elevated punning into a literary technique—as a most important source of inspiration" (Schwarz, p. 80). It was Brisset who in the first years of the twentieth century anticipated Structuralism by analyzing the phonetic and lexical relationships of words in different languages. And in one of the later notes for *The Green Box* Duchamp writes:

> Take a Larousse dictionary and copy all the so-called "abstract" words.
> i.e.
> those which have no concrete reference.
>> Compose a schematic sign designating each of these words. (this sign can be composed with the standard-stops)
>> These signs must be thought of as the letters of the new alphabet
>> (Duchamp, Hamilton, and Hamilton)

In the lines that follow, Duchamp suggests a kind of grammar and syntax for the construction of nonverbal propositions, to be used as the theoretical basis for a plastic language. If puns, anagrams, and alliterations are the lowest literary forms, they also represent some of the building blocks which constitute an important element in twentieth-century literature. In such a way split and multiple verbal meanings account for the ready-mades and Duchamp's quasi-conceptual works of art.

From our analysis of *The Large Glass* and its notes, it seems more than likely that Duchamp arrived at a semiological theory of modern art as early as 1912. How much of it was artistic vision and how much intellectual deduction remains open to question. Yet acceptance of this possibility best explains the artist's subsequent secrecy and semiretirement from art. Duchamp's obvious aim after 1912 was to establish the most distant limits of art; anything accomplished after that he understood as so much repetition and elaboration.

Much of what Duchamp had labored so long to tell us—albeit in the context of a series of riddles and myths—is similar to what Lévi-Strauss has tried to convey. The sum of the message is that Western culture is well on the way to dissolution because of technological hubris and self-delusion. Applying the same standards of change to art and to science can only precipitate the destruction of myths and sign systems. Duchamp implies that Thanatos rather than Eros dominates our cultural games. For Lévi-Strauss myths remain a cohesive force reminding men that they are neither wild animals nor machines, but something consciously and precariously removed from both. With the collapse of mythic structures and totemic systems men lose their conceptual security. They are, so to speak, placed at the mercy of Nature and their own animal desires. What remains is a random assortment of entities, materials, processes, and synthetic concepts—the "junk of life" in Duchamp's phraseology.

Perhaps this is the meaning behind the artist's last major work, the strange *tableau vivant* in the Philadelphia Museum entitled *Given: 1. The Waterfall/ 2. The Illuminating Gas* (1946–1966). One looks through two tiny peepholes in a permanently closed set of weather-beaten doors. The scene within recapitulates the Bride's final achievement of orgasm. She lies among twigs and dried leaves, illuminating her debauched position with a gas lamp held aloft. This lifelike figure suffers the loss of a right arm and two feet, while her head is obscured from view. The gas lamp and a waterfall remain symbols of castration. In dioramic form the background provides an idyllic forest scene, painted in a misty *trompe l'œil* manner not unlike the mysterious landscapes of Leonardo's paintings. With the ultimate coming together of the Bride's Waterfall and the Bachelors' Illuminating Gas, the Bride is stripped and ravished—but in an utterly literal and realistic fashion. It is as if Duchamp is graphically telling us that modern art is a circular path, leading us back, not to the realism of the Renaissance, but rather to life itself—to confrontation of the human animal with itself.

V

Epilogue

The first result of our substitution is very remarkable. If the totem animal is the father, then the two main commandments of totemism, the two taboo rules which constitute its nucleus—not to kill the totem animal and not to use a woman belonging to the same totem for sexual purposes—agree in content with the two crimes of Oedipus, who slew his father and took his mother to wife, and also with the child's two primal wishes whose insufficient represssion or whose reawakening forms the nucleus of perhaps all neuroses.

—SIGMUND FREUD
Totem and Taboo

OEDIPUS COMPLETE

The cornerstone of *The Large Glass,* and possibly all modern artistic creativity, appears to be the fable of Oedipus. As with all myths, the plot of Oedipus and the Sphinx varies from writer to writer. In its essential form Laius, King of Thebes, is warned by the Delphic oracle that he will suffer death at the hands of a future son, whom, when born, the king reluctantly orders given to a herdsman to be destroyed. The herdsman takes pity on the infant and leaves him alive, suspended from the branch of a tree. He is found and raised in the house of the King of Corinth as the monarch's son, given the name Oedipus, or Swollen-foot.

As a young man Oedipus exiles himself from Corinth when an oracle tells him that he will murder his father, whom he believes to be Polybus, King of Corinth. In his travels Oedipus encounters another chariot on the road and quarrels with its driver over the right of way. In provoked anger he slays the driver and a passenger who, unknown to Oedipus, is his true father, King Laius.

Before the murder of Laius, the city of Thebes had been placed under siege by a fearful man-eater, a monster with the body of a winged lion and the face and breasts of a woman. Travelers to and from the city were challenged by this animal, called the Sphinx, to solve a riddle. And since no wayfarer had successfully answered her question, all were devoured. When Oedipus confronts the Sphinx and is asked, "What animal is that which in the morning goes on four feet, at noon on two, and in the evening upon three?" Oedipus answers, "Man. In childhood he creeps on hands and knees, in manhood walks erect, and in old age with the aid of a staff." The answer is exactly right and this so demolishes the Sphinx that she commits suicide.

In joyous appreciation, the citizens of Thebes crown Oedipus their king and award him with the hand of the widowed Queen Jocasta. Not only has the original prediction fulfilled itself, but Oedipus has also married his own mother. For many years the city of Thebes prospers and the royal pair produce two sons and two daughters. Eventually plague and famine descend. The city is near ruin when Oedipus is told by the oracle that to lift the curse he must find his father's murderer. He then learns that he himself had committed the crime. Jocasta also learns the truth and commits suicide. Oedipus blinds himself and lives out his life as a wretched wanderer, cared for only by his daughters.

In his *Structural Anthropology* Lévi-Strauss treats the Oedipus myth as a four-part invention (1958, pp. 213–18). He divides the myth's text (more extended than the above version) into four topical columns consisting of: *overrated blood relations, underrated blood relations, denial of man's autochthonous (unisexual) origins,* and *persistence of his autochthonous origins.* The problem as Edmund Leach established it in his elegant analysis of the Biblical story of Genesis is that of "patrilineal descent: the requirement that fathers shall be perpetuated in their sons without the intervention of women, which in simple fact is plainly impossible" (Hayes and Hayes, p. 52). Myths, then, according to Leach's interpretation of Lévi-Strauss, reorganize reality along the lines of seemingly logical models. They evade biological truths by providing conceptual continuity between life as we would like to see it and the inevitability of reproduction, old age, and death. Lévi-Strauss's four columns represent such a mediation. Oedipus's incestual marriage represents overrated blood relations, while the murder of his father represents underrated (or unhonored) blood relations. With the other two columns, it is less evident that the destruction of the Sphinx signifies a denial of man's autochthonous origins, or that Oedipus's lameness is the persistence of patrilineal descent. But approximating Leach's diagram of the relationships established by Lévi-Strauss, the connection between the columns becomes more obvious.

$$\frac{\text{Jocasta/Oedipus}}{\text{Laius/Oedipus}} = \frac{\text{incest}}{\text{patricide}} = \text{Sphinx}$$

Oedipus assumes the honorable task of eliminating the Sphinx which in mythic form represents the fusion of his parents. According to Leach, "He accomplishes this end by sinning doubly—incest with Jocasta and patricide against Laius" (Hayes and Hayes, p. 52). Thus in Freudian terms how could the son take the father's place with the mother except by literally replacing the father? In terms of genetics and chronology, not to speak of incest taboos, this is impossible; but in fact it occurs every time a son takes a wife and becomes a father himself. So in reality the myth mediates a time gap and also those psychological attachments between children and parents. The Sphinx then is Time and the persistence of genealogical ties. Oedipus is lame or "incomplete" because he can only assume the position of his father by becoming a father himself. Just as he is too close to his mother and desirous of his father's death, the Sphinx assumes the over-completeness of hermaphroditic existence, and Oedipus the incompleteness of a man who has not replaced himself.

As a biological paradigm, the Oedipus myth represents a key relationship in all evolutionary procedures involving human beings. In fact it regulates historical thought. Like Oedipus, each rising generation of history-oriented artists is confronted with the ambivalent need to produce art as their predecessors did, yet create an art which is entirely new in style and esthetic conception. This exactly parallels Lévi-Strauss's juxtaposition of underrated and overrated blood relations. All young artists feel constrained by history to reject the styles of past artists; at the same time they are forced to create something which is structurally consistent with all former principles of art. For the artist the Sphinx is Art History, combining the enigma of overattraction and overrejection. Great artists—in the light of history—produce a maximum combination of both effects. Thus the artist is complete *as an artist* when he has solved the Sphinx's riddle, and becomes himself a part of Art History.

Duchamp's fierce iconoclasm led the artist to the same conclusion when he investigated the limits of artistic principles through optical and mechanical experiments in the 1920's. He implied as much in his short lecture, "The Creative Act," which he gave in April, 1957. On several levels he indicates the congruence between creativity and the Oedipus myth.

> Consequently, in the chain of reactions accompanying the creative act, a link is missing. This gap, representing the inability of the artist to express fully his intention, this difference between what he intended to realize and did realize, is the personal "art coefficient" contained in the work.

In other words, the personal "art coefficient" is like the arithmetical relation between the unexpressed but intended and the unintentionally expressed (Lebel, p. 78).

On the Oedipal plane, the "unexpressed but intended" is the unexpressed hostility of Oedipus for his father; the "unintentionally expressed" is the son making love to his mother. Viewed as creative metaphors, the first relates to the artist's tacit rejection of past art (not in principle but as a model to emulate on the visual level) through the invention of a unique artistic discovery or style. However, by making art he is forced to do what all previous artists have done (incest), and this unintentionally expresses the inevitability of his position. In this decade we are beset by many examples of artists striving for a total "art of immateriality" or for an artistic expression doing away with art altogether. Such negative tendencies are inevitable as avant-garde art drops its normal signifiers and is forced to rely on rhetoric and end-game dialectical strategies to perpetuate itself.

This appears in the Duchampian pun *Incest ou passion de famille/ A coups trop tirés* which terminates with the remark, "Shot off too many times" or "Printed too many times." Here we need an alchemical explanation in terms of family relationships for the four-part matrix of the Real System. The Plane of Content is defined by a signifier (Mother) and a signified (Father), just as the Plane of Expression reveals a signifier (Daughter) and a signified (Son). Making too much avant-garde art results in a situation where the Son and Daughter form a family without the Father and Mother (nonobjective art). Duchamp constantly warns us that neither *incest* (making mistructured art) nor *promiscuity* (relying on past art or the effects of randomness) will lead to an understanding of the mechanisms underlying semiotic systems in general. Neither do these habits lead to equilibrium in the personality; this is the greater message of the creator of *The Large Glass*.

Another interpretation of the *Glass* allegorically uses the numerical symbolism of the Oedipus myth. Sophocles in *Oedipus Rex* consistently employs the sacred triad, three and multiples of three, as Duchamp does in the *Glass*. The number three stands for the third age of man in the Sphinx's riddle, and also for resurrection and enlightenment. Aristotle showed that two terms were insufficient and four terms unnecessary to produce a rigorous syllogism. In Structuralism the trichotomy, thesis-antithesis-synthesis, represents the dialectic of all systems involved in evolutionary change. Genetically, the Aristotelian logic structure represents the solution to the Oedipus Myth.

The Nine Malic Molds are perhaps Duchamp's rejection of all past art and artists, while the androgynous character of the Milky Way or Top Inscription is no doubt identifiable with the Sphinx. We must not forget that the scissors and bayonet of the Bachelor Machine reflect the castration complex suffered by Duchamp as an Oedipal figure. The artist's partial renunciation of art denotes a kind of blindness; relevant in this case are Duchamp's remarks about the futility of creating more "retinal" art. Nevertheless Duchamp, with the *Boîte-en-valise* and other projects recapitulating his artistic metamorphosis, makes certain that we understand that it is he who first broke the Sphinx's riddle.

Taking a larger view of the Duchampian myth, it recapitulates the demise of matriarchal traditions in a patriarchal society. According to the pioneer psychoanalyst Otto Rank (Mullahy, pp. 168–76), the Greek artist discovered idealization by identifying with the mother *as a mutual creator*. This again alludes to a concurrent longing for and hateful rejection of "the bestial womb." The achievement of artistic recognition gives the artist not only the power of historical conquest over the father, but the experience of having rejoined the mother in a prenatal and hence sexual capacity. If it refers to any single circumstance, *The Large Glass* is a metaphor for the modern obsession of *violent* and *conclusive* conquest over the father; or specifically, killing the father inevitably results in destruction of the mother.

Removed to a still larger scale, it explains the ultimate differences between matriarchal and patriarchal societies. Being synchronic, matriarchies are oriented toward stability and permanence; their institutions of kinship and passive acceptance of nature's ways help to define human life as the highest value. This is in contrast to patriarchal societies where a respect for legal structures, political hierarchies, and rational thought as a form of domination over nature prevail through powerful states administered by varying degrees of repression. Repression itself stems from an inability to cope with painful memories of the birth trauma, reinstituted by Duchamp in the Bride's Waterfall. This provokes increasing exclusion, not only of women, but of the institutions represented by them. Therefore we have a situation today in which intensified dehumanization of the environment is met in a multitude of weaker forms representing the mother principle. Alignment of forces on both sides is obvious. Domination by the patriarchal order has moved civilization within an inch of extinction; circumstances are already moving us in the other direction.

So the execution of the Bride, first by Duchamp and then by the avant-garde, alludes to the curious murder or suicide of Jocasta. Jocasta is the mother principle who fails by condoning the death of her child Oedipus in order to save her husband. Significantly her crime is laudable from a patriarchal point of view. Interpreted in immediate terms, this study represents the killing of art through intellectual comprehension. By further undermining the father's rule, it perpetuates the tyranny of the patriarchal principle. Oedipus symbolizes victorious individualism or immortality awarded the privilege of incest. But victory is meaningless, as Duchamp indicated, when it represents destroying the prize signifying victory. The alternative is renunciation of victory and all of its implications.

ART DEGREE ZERO

Unavoidably, all languages and other sign systems preclude metaphysical premises. Roland Barthes repeatedly asserts that signs remain "open" and by necessity unverifiable. So it seems that every social institution, from religion to traffic regulations, operates as a communication mode with no more authority than the rules of speech. What gives such institutions their power over our lives is their *consistency.* Whatever is done within a semiotic system is always structurally consistent with what has gone before. The pattern of concepts is recognizable because it proceeds with reference to its own past. It is this repetition abetted by a proscribed order that defines man's connection to and separation from nature.

Obviously the major semiotic traditions—religion, philosophy, art, and architecture—no longer serve to integrate society with the natural order. Art is irrevocably divorced from present technology, or for that matter from all essential intellectual activity. The art impulse, as we have seen, is virtually a parody of its former self. And doubtless it is the domination of patriarchal institutions that accounts for the overall rejection of art as an economic luxury and unnecessary metaphysical baggage. On the other hand, it is the artist's and art historian's inability to understand the nature of art that prevents them from projecting art into all aspects of life, as an approach to living. Thus the dehumanizing effects of technology continue with no adequate answer as to why they are so consistently lethal. We refuse to accept the reality that technologies preclude the use of myth and ritual just as art now does. However, the difference is that scientific tools only allow us to *culturalize the natural,* never the reverse. Very conceivably biological survival depends upon *naturalization of the cultural* as well. Yet it is acutely apparent that few if any of our social agencies have the capacity to incorporate both procedures into their structures. There was a time, even prior to the Renaissance, when art and science were compatible. One great example of such "ecumenical art" is described in detail by Gerald S. Hawkins in his book *Stonehenge Decoded.* In this instance the word "art" is used deliberately to define what it is for

45. Stonehenge, *Salisbury Plain, England. New Stone Age, c. 1800–1400* B.C. *British Crown Copyright. Photograph courtesy Ministry of Public Building and Works, London.*

people who build and experience universalizing institutions, and not to denote sites or objects of high archeological or museological interest.

In the 1950's Hawkins, a professor of astronomy, began to explore the Stonehenge site located near Amesbury in southern England. For hundreds of years Stonehenge was believed to be a Druid temple. But Hawkins's investigations during the early 1960's and his papers "Stonehenge Decoded" (appearing in *Nature,* October 26, 1963) and "Stonehenge: A Neolithic Computer" (appearing in *Nature,* June 27, 1964) proved rather conclusively that the site is a 3,500-year-old astronomical observatory.

In plan Stonehenge consists of six concentric configurations: the outer two are circles of holes; the next, being the most regular and obvious, is the columns and lintels of the sarsen circle; within this is the much smaller bluestone circle; and in the center are the five giant trilithons and bluestone horseshoes. The two horseshoes line up with a point on the horizon where the midsummer sunrise occurs. The larger stones weigh from 20 to 50 tons apiece; consequently one of the most fascinating aspects of Stonehenge is the speculation of how a portion of these monoliths were transported three hundred miles to their final destination.

Some obvious alignments impelled Hawkins to believe that there might be further sun-moon alignments between the archways of the sarsen circle and the trilithons. Even with many of the original monoliths lost or misplaced in reconstruction, the astronomer discovered that there are at least twelve significant alignments each for the sun and the moon, defined by the minima and maxima declinations of these celestial bodies. Subsequently, Hawkins proposed a theory that the holes surrounding the sarsen circle, with the aid of marking stones, were used as a computer to predict years of eclipse or seasons when the moon is visible through various apertures of sight. Notably, all of Hawkins's discoveries were vastly facilitated by a high-speed digital computer.

Still and all, this brief description does not begin to impart the remarkable intellectual skill involved in the planning of this edifice. Maneuvering thirty-ton monoliths, the artist-scientists of Stonehenge lined up axes of sight for dozens of celestial positions, without the use of modern surveying instruments or engineering equipment. The entire project spanned four or five hundred years, ending around 1500 B.C. Yet what did it mean? This is Hawkins's opinion:

> The Stonehenge sun-moon alignments were created and elaborated for two, possibly three, reasons: they made a calendar, particularly useful to tell the time for planting crops; they helped to create and maintain priestly power, by enabling the priest to call out the multitude to see the spectacular risings and settings of the sun and moon, most especially the midsummer sunrise over the heel stone and midwinter sunset through the great trilithon, and possibly they served as an intellectual game (Hawkins, p. 117).

Strangely, the astronomer's references also echo Duchamp's subtitle for *The Bride Stripped Bare by Her Bachelors, Even,* in which he called the *Glass* an "Agricultural machine" or "Apparatus, instrument for farming." Did Duchamp have some inclination of art's prehistoric purposes (its use in farming, hunting, and lawmaking), or was he simply a priest with the power to end the priesthood? Stonehenge was nevertheless far more vital than the Glass Bead Game. Notably this ancient English calendar involved the labor of thousands of people over several centuries. In mediating cultural and natural elements Stonehenge assumes all the prerequisites of a work of art. If an artist were to design a monumental work embodying the greatest possible union between man's position on Earth and the cyclical events of the chief celestial bodies, the obvious choice would be some variation of this edifice.

We have seen that the language of relationships within the visual arts has steadily deteriorated to the extent that it exists in only the most transparent terms. Art as we know it is bound to disappear shortly. But what actually is dying: a social order or a specific set of myths? More than likely the answer is both. In her recent book, *Natural Symbols,* the anthropologist Mary Douglas alludes to the fact that the symbols of art are another measure of the strength of ritual in a society, although the two are by no means congruent. As forms of signification are discarded, ritual differentiation between the role of an artist and other members of society has gradually faded, as has the idea that art contains some particular efficacy, magical or otherwise. Moreover, avant-garde art is probably the first instance in which artistic expression is programmatically destroyed by artists in the name of "visual exploration," which is hardly surprising since this term is a surrogate for the scientific impulse. In Dr. Douglas's words:

> We are then able to see that alienation from the current social values usually takes a set form: a denunciation not only of irrelevant rituals, but of ritualism as such; exaltation of the inner experience and denigration of its standard expressions; preference for intuitive and instant forms of knowledge; rejection of any tendency to allow habit to provide the basis of a new symbolic system. *In its extreme forms antiritualism is an attempt to abolish communication by means of complex symbolic systems* (Douglas, p. 19, italics added).

It follows that her last sentence also pertains to science. The most obvious consequence of demythification is that, once begun, it probably will not stop until the entire semiological infrastructure of the present society is uprooted. Just as it denies history, Structuralism is paradoxically a tool of historical change.

One of the truisms of Structuralism is that myths mirror or recapitulate the social structure supporting them. The fact that art has its "patrons," "benefactors," and "tastemakers" simply informs us that once out of the hands of the artists, art acts as a kind of social counter or signal denoting status and financial worth. In centuries past art's function was to act as a medium for religious or political ideologies. Today the acquisition of valuable art is in itself an ideological act. Mythologically, this financial quantification of the art impulse is simply an extension of the underlying value system, just as works of art are considered "priceless" only in the sense that any object, once awarded a niche in art history, is irreplaceable to the myth. The real purpose of art's costliness is to make us aware of the benevolences and merits of those who control art patronage.

Until recently artists operated ambivalently as martyrs and eccentrics, symbols in a society absolving itself by occasionally buying a transubstantiated piece of the artist. This was true even as Albert Aurier wrote in 1890 that "The painter's subject is in himself. . . . All spectacles, all emotions, all dreams resolve themselves for him into combinations of patches; into relationships of tones and tints; into lines" (Gimpel, p. 143). And since the early nineteenth century the greatest artists have made essentially autobiographical art. Such personalism reached its logical conclusion when a few artists today simply document their own bodily activities. In its final stages, this represents the termination of the iconic impulse. Even attempts to buy or underwrite Earth Art or Conceptual Art only stress the fact that the collector is willing to pay for his own demise. But just as inevitably the production of "normal" modern art will continue. For how long and under what circumstances is still a matter of speculation.

While the collector and artist are clan members in danger of losing their totemic system, it is difficult to believe that such a concept will not be replaced by something much more essential to contemporary life. Marshall McLuhan is perhaps the first interpreter of communication to understand what these changes involve: "It is well to disabuse ourselves of the 'sense of myth' as unreal or false. It was the fragmented and literate intellectualism of the Greeks that destroyed the integral mythic vision to which we are now returning. . . ." (McLuhan, p. 185). Most probably the new myths will be scientifically oriented, but devoid of the emotional aridity and repressiveness which so many people associate with present scientific methods.

We are witnessing the death throes of the classical art impulse and more than likely the birth of a totally new understanding of the social use of sign systems. Structuralism itself seems to be a dialectical device for removing mankind from the lingering influences of Classicism. Ideal time and scientific experimental idealism remain outgrowths of the classical frame of reference. They stem from the intuition that location and proportion transcend the illusion of time, thus embodying the myth of art as well. In both classical artistic and scientific experimentation the strictest control is exacted over the ordering of isolated but complementary relationships. Reduction, isolation, and manipulation are the foundations of the classic inventive structure in art or technology.

It is now possible to understand the importance of gravitational effects upon the mythic structure of art. Classical and Newtonian physics held that a body persists in a state of rest or constant motion except when affected by other bodies; the *normal* condition of all things being inertia. Classicism embodies the Western ideal of constancy. In contrast the art historical myth asserts that materially things change, but psychically we remain the same. Yet since the beginning of this century, Einsteinian physics has insisted that all bodies are constantly being affected by other bodies; their normal condition is continuous motion and change. So it is obvious that the twentieth century represents an enormously violent rupture between synchronic and diachronic habits of thought. As yet there are few if any diachronic traditions not absolutely disastrous to the welfare of society as a whole. We live one way but think another. But a few thoughtful historians have already disavowed most of the illusions of history as measures of change. From the vantage point of natural science, the idea of *informational and technical complexity* represents one of the only creditable criteria of mutability. However, cultural complexity—if we accept the Western standard of technical sophistication—may only be obtained by depleting existing ecosystems and biosystems. In other words, we seem to develop new modes of technology at the expense of surrounding environmental systems, including ourselves. Thus it remains to be seen if this one criterion of change, complexity, is more than another postclassical illusion.

Art is disappearing because the old separations between nature and culture no longer have any classification value. Biology tells us that what is cultural *is* ultimately natural or it does not survive. Ecologists insist that what is natural must become an integral and valued part of our culture. All classification systems require a division of the world. Obviously the basic social revolutions currently under way present us with an extremely altered set of divisions, implying new priorities and patterns of existence. If in Lévi-Strauss's terms *humanization of the natural* implies religion, and *naturalization of the cultural* implies magic, this should not threaten our sense of rationality nor prevent us from understanding that the two processes are an integral and natural function of human thought—both previously and for the future. Religion and magic are simply pejorative expressions for mental processes with exhausted content. Quite likely we are already formulating more suitable epistomological structures embodying the functions of religion and magic. These will be considered eminently logical and praiseworthy. *If he understands his work, and the fact that it no longer demands mystification, the artist can still be a tremendously valuable figure in society.*

It appears that we have come full circle. Classicism has ceased because the center of artistic gravity is a mythical degree zero in space-time. We have reached that point. One remembers one of the notes placed by Marcel Duchamp in *The Green Box:*

> Regime of Coincidence
> Ministry of gravity

Then Duchamp supplies directions for a painting or sculpture: "Flat container. in glass—[holding] all sorts of liquids. Colored, pieces of wood, of iron, chemical reactions. Shape the container. and look through it—."

"Coincidence" in this instance relates to the ambiguity between natural and cultural elements subjected to the most random and offhand methods of alteration by the artist. "Gravity" of course is the ultimate force controlling all naturalizing effects. Duchamp's liquid-filled construction represents the randomization of artistic order—a work of art which is neither this nor that, art whose intentionality lies in its ambiguity and lack of a second signified. Together the two phrases signify the termination of artistic logic, art degree zero.

Possibly we are witnessing the Global Village in its first stages of development. Since art has reached Duchamp's Jura Mountains, perhaps we are already on the moon, and looking back from that vantage point we see only overall patterns and a totality of existence on the Earth that was never before available for our perception. Having long been shocked by the separateness of things, peoples, cities, countries, and continents, these premonitions appear hopeful.

Bibliography

AGEE, WILLIAM C., with Notes by Dan Flavin and Selected Writings by the Artist (February 27–March 24, 1968). *Don Judd,* exhibition catalogue (New York: Whitney Museum of American Art).

ALLOWAY, LAWRENCE (September–October, 1963). *Morris Louis: 1912–1962, Memorial Exhibition Paintings from 1954 to 1960,* exhibition catalogue (New York: The Solomon R. Guggenheim Museum).

————— (1966). *Systemic Painting,* exhibition catalogue (New York: The Solomon R. Guggenheim Museum).

ARNASON, H. H. (1968). *History of Modern Art: Painting, Sculpture, Architecture* (Englewood Cliffs, N. J.: Prentice-Hall, and New York: Harry N. Abrams).

ARNHEIM, RUDOLF (1954). *Art and Visual Perception* (Berkeley and Los Angeles: University of California Press, 1969).

————— (1969). *Visual Thinking* (Berkeley and Los Angeles: University of California Press).

Art-Language (February, 1970). Vol. 1, No. 2 (Chipping Norton, England: Art and Language Press).

BARTHES, ROLAND (1953). *Writing Degree Zero and Elements of Semiology,* translated by Annette Lavers and Colin Smith (Boston: Beacon Press, 1970).

————— (1967). *Système de la mode* (Paris: Éditions du Seuil).

BEARDLEY, MOLLY, and HITCHFIELD, ELIZABETH (1966). *A Guide to Reading Piaget* (New York: Schocken Books, 1969).

BERENSON, BERNARD (1948). *Aesthetics and History* (Garden City, N.Y.: Doubleday Anchor Books, Doubleday and Company, 1954).

BINFORD, SALLY R., and BINFORD, LEWIS R. (eds.) (1965). *New Perspectives in Archeology* (Chicago: Aldine Publishing Company and the University of New Mexico).

BRILL, DR. A. A. (translated and edited by, with an introduction by) (1938). *The Basic Writings of Sigmund Freud* (New York: The Modern Library, Random House).

Bulfinch's Mythology (1964). (London: Spring Books).

BUREN, DANIEL (March, 1970). "Beware!" (London: *Studio International*), pp. 100–04.

BURNHAM, JACK (1968). *Beyond Modern Sculpture: The Effects of Science and Technology on the Sculpture of This Century* (New York: George Braziller).

———— (September, 1969). "Real Time Systems" (New York: *Artforum*), pp. 49–55.

BURY, J. B. (1932). *The Idea of Progress* (New York: Dover Publications, 1960).

CANADAY, JOHN (1959). *Mainstreams of Modern Art* (New York: Holt, Rinehart and Winston, 1964).

CARROLL, LEWIS (1865, 1871). *The Annotated Alice: Alice's Adventures in Wonderland & Through the Looking Glass,* with an Introduction and Notes by Martin Gardner (New York: Clarkson N. Potter, 1960).

CELANT, GERMANO (1969). *Art Povera* (New York: Frederick A. Praeger).

CHIPP, HERSCHEL B., with contributions by Peter Selz and Joshua C. Taylor (1968). *Theories of Modern Art: A Source Book by Artists and Critics* (Berkeley and Los Angeles: University of California Press, 1969).

CHOMSKY, NOAM (1968). *Language and Mind* (New York: Harcourt, Brace and World).

DOUGLAS, MARY (1970). *Natural Symbols: Explorations in Cosmology* (New York: Pantheon Books).

DUCHAMP, MARCEL (1960). *The Bride Stripped Bare by Her Bachelors, Even (The Green Box),* translated by George Heard Hamilton; Richard Hamilton (ed.) (New York: George Wittenborn).

FRIED, MICHAEL (Summer, 1967). "Art and Objecthood" (New York: *Artforum*), pp. 12–23.

FRY, EDWARD F. (1969). *David Smith,* exhibition catalogue (New York: The Solomon R. Guggenheim Museum).

GEIST, SIDNEY (1967). *Brancusi: A Study of the Sculpture* (New York: Grossman, 1968).

———— (1969). *Constantin Brancusi 1876–1957: A Retrospective Exhibition,* exhibition catalogue (New York: The Solomon R. Guggenheim Museum).

GIMPEL, JEAN (1968). *The Cult of Art,* translated from the French (New York: Stein and Day, 1969).

GOOSSEN, E. C. (1968). *The Art of the Real: USA 1948–1968,* exhibition catalogue (New York: The Museum of Modern Art).

GORDON, JOHN (1968). *Franz Kline: 1910–1962,* exhibition catalogue (New York: Whitney Museum of American Art).

GRAY, CLEVE (ed.) (1968). *David Smith by David Smith* (New York: Holt, Rinehart and Winston).

HAMILTON, GEORGE HEARD (1954). *Manet and his Critics* (London: Geoffrey Cumberledge, Oxford University Press).

———, and AGEE, WILLIAM C. (1967). *Raymond Duchamp-Villon* (New York: Walker and Company).

HAWKINS, GERALD S., in collaboration with John B. White (1965). *Stonehenge Decoded* (New York: Dell Publishing Co.).

HAYES, E. NELSON, and HAYES, TANYA (eds.) (1970). *Claude Lévi-Strauss: The Anthropologist as Hero* (Cambridge: The M.I.T. Press).

HERBERT, ROBERT L. (ed.) (1964). *The Art Criticism of John Ruskin* (Garden City, N. Y.: Doubleday Anchor Books, Doubleday and Company).

——— (ed.) (1964). *Modern Artists On Art: Ten Unabridged Essays* (Englewood Cliffs, N. J.: Prentice-Hall).

——— (1968). *Neo-Impressionism,* exhibition catalogue (New York: The Solomon R. Guggenheim Museum).

HESS, THOMAS B. (1959). *Willem de Kooning* (New York: George Braziller).

HESSE, HERMANN (1943). *The Glass Bead Game (Magister Ludi),* translated by Richard and Clara Winston (New York: Holt, Rinehart and Winston, 1969; London: Jonathan Cape Ltd.).

HOMER, WILLIAM INNES (1964). *Seurat and the Science of Painting* (Cambridge: The M.I.T. Press).

JUDD, DONALD (1965). "Specific Objects" in *Contemporary Sculpture,* Arts Yearbook No. 8 (New York: *The Art Digest*), pp. 74–82.

KANDINSKY, WASSILY (1947). *Concerning the Spiritual in Art and Painting in Particular 1912,* The Documents of Modern Art, Vol. 5 (New York: George Wittenborn, 1970).

KARSHAN, DONALD (April 10–August 25, 1970). *Conceptual Art and Conceptual Aspects,* exhibition catalogue (New York: The New York Cultural Center).

KLEE, PAUL (1961). *Paul Klee: The Thinking Eye,* translated by Ralph Manheim with assistance from Dr. Charlotte Weidler and Joyce Wittenborn, Jürg Spiller (ed.) (London: Lund Humphries; New York: George Wittenborn).

KOZLOFF, MAX (1967). *Jasper Johns* (New York: Harry N. Abrams).

KUBLER, GEORGE (1962). *The Shape of Time* (New Haven and London: Yale University Press, 1968).

LEACH, EDMUND (ed.) (1967). *The Structural Study of Myth and Totemism* (London: Tavistock Publications, 1968; Social Science Paperback, 1968).

———— (1970). *Claude Lévi-Strauss,* Modern Masters (New York: Viking Press).

LEBEL, ROBERT (1959). *Marcel Duchamp,* translated by George Heard Hamilton (New York: Grove Press).

LÉVI-STRAUSS, CLAUDE (1962a). *The Savage Mind* (Chicago: The University of Chicago Press, 1966; London: George Weidenfeld & Nicolson Ltd.).

———— (1962b). *Totemism,* translated by Rodney Needham (Boston: Beacon Press, 1963).

———— (1963). *Structural Anthropology,* translated by Claire Jacobson and Brooke Grundfest Schoepf (New York: Basic Books).

———— (1964). *The Raw and the Cooked: Introduction to a Science of Mythology: I,* translated by John and Doreen Weightman (New York: Harper Torchbooks, Harper and Row; London: Jonathan Cape Ltd.).

———— (1967). *The Scope of Anthropology,* translated by Sherry Ortner, Paul and Robert A. Paul (London: Jonathan Cape Ltd.).

LIPPARD, LUCY R., with contributions by Lawrence Alloway, Nancy Marmer, Nicolas Calas (1966). *Pop Art* (New York: Frederick A. Praeger).

MALEVICH, KASIMIR S. (Vol. I, 1915–1928; Vol. II, 1928–1933). *Essays on Art,* translated by Xenia Glowacki-Prus and Arnold McMillin; Troels Andersen (ed.) (Copenhagen: Borgen, 1968).

———— (1927). *The Non-Objective World,* translated by Howard Dearstyne (Chicago: Paul Theobald and Company, 1959).

MATSON, FLOYD W. (1964). *The Broken Image: Man, Science and Society* (Garden City, N. Y.: Doubleday Anchor Books, Doubleday and Company, 1966).

McLUHAN, MARSHALL, and FIORE, QUENTIN, coordinated by Jerome Agel (1968). *War and Peace in the Global Village* (New York: McGraw Hill Book Company).

MEYERHOFF, HANS (An anthology selected by, with an Introduction and Commentary by) (1959). *The Philosophy of History in Our Time* (Garden City, N. Y.: Doubleday Anchor Books, Doubleday and Company).

MICHELSON, ANNETTE (November 24–December 28, 1969). *Robert Morris,* exhibition catalogue (Washington: The Corcoran Gallery of Art).

MONDRIAN, PIET (1945). *Plastic Art and Pure Plastic Art 1937 and Other Essays, 1941–1943,* The Documents of Modern Art (New York: Wittenborn, Schultz, 3rd ed., 1951).

MONTE, JAMES, and TUCKER, MARCIA (May 19, 1969–July 6, 1969). *Anti-Illusion: Procedures/Materials,* exhibition catalogue (New York: Whitney Museum of American Art).

MORRIS, ROBERT (April, 1970). "Some Notes on the Phenomenology of Making" (New York: *Artforum*), pp. 62–66.

MULLAHY, PATRICK (1948). *Oedipus: Myth and Complex: A Review of Psychoanalytic Theory* (New York: Grove Press, 1955).

MURRAY, HENRY A. (ed.) (1959). *Myth and Mythmaking* (Boston: Beacon Press, 1968).

NIETZSCHE, FRIEDRICH (1901). *The Will to Power,* translated by Walter Kaufmann and R. J. Hollingdale (New York: Random House, 1960).

O'HARA, FRANK (1959). *Jackson Pollock* (New York: George Braziller).

PANOFSKY, ERWIN (1924). *Idea: A Concept in Art Theory,* translated by Joseph J. S. Peake (Columbia: University of South Carolina Press, 1968).

PAZ, OCTAVIO (1968–70). *Marcel Duchamp or The Castle of Purity,* translated by Donald Gardner (London: Cape Goliard Press in association with Grossman, New York, 1970).

PECKHAM, MORSE (1965). *Man's Rage for Chaos* (New York: Schocken Books, 1967).

PIAGET, JEAN (1970). *Genetic Epistemology,* translated by Eleanor Duckworth (New York: Columbia University Press).

—— and INHELDER, BÄRBEL (1948). *The Child's Conception of Space,* translated by F. J. Langdon and J. L. Lunzer (New York: W. W. Norton and Company, 1967).

PINCUS-WITTEN, ROBERT (September, 1969). "Slow Information: Richard Serra" (New York: *Artforum*), pp. 34–39.

PLATO. *Phaedo,* translated by R. S. Block (London: Routledge and Kegan Paul, 1955).

READ, HERBERT (ed.) (1934). *Unit 1: The Modern Movement in English Architecture, Painting, and Sculpture* (London: Cassell and Company).

—— (1959). *A Concise History of Modern Painting* (New York: Frederick A. Praeger, 3rd printing, 1964).

ROBERTSON, BRIAN (1960). *Jackson Pollock* (New York: Harry N. Abrams).

ROSE, BARBARA (1967). *American Art Since 1900: A Critical History* (New York: Frederick A. Praeger).

―――― (ed.) (1968). *Readings in American Art Since 1900* (New York: Frederick A. Praeger).

RUSSELL, JOHN (1965). *Seurat* (New York: Frederick A. Prager).

SAUSSURE, FERDINAND DE (1915). *Course in General Linguistics,* translated by Wade Baskin, Charles Bally, and Albert Sechehaye (eds.), in collaboration with Albert Reidlinger (New York: Philosophical Library, 1959).

SCHAPIRO, MEYER (1953). "Style", in *Aesthetics Today*. Readings selected, edited, and introduced by Morris Philipson (Cleveland and New York: Meridian Books, The World Publishing Company, 1961), pp. 81–113.

SCHWARZ, ARTURO (1969). *The Complete Works of Marcel Duchamp* (New York: Harry N. Abrams).

SCOTT, IAN A. (ed. and trans.) (1969). Based on the original German text by Dr. Max Lüscher (1948). *The Lüscher Color Test* (New York: Random House).

SEGALL, H. MARSHALL; CAMPBELL, DONALD T.; and HERSKOVITS, MELVILLE J. (1966). *The Influence of Culture on Visual Perception* (Indianapolis, New York, Kansas City: The Bobbs-Merrill Co.).

SMITH, BRYDON (organizer) (1969). *fluorescent light, etc. from Dan Flavin,* exhibition catalogue (Ottawa: Published by the National Gallery of Canada for the Queen's Printer).

SOLOMON, ALAN R. (February 16–April 12, 1964). *Jasper Johns,* exhibition catalogue (New York: The Jewish Museum).

SYPHER, WYLIE (ed.) (1963). *Art History: An Anthology of Modern Criticism* (New York: Vintage Books, Random House).

TUCHMAN, PHYLLIS (June, 1970). "An Interview with Carl Andre" (New York: *Artforum*), pp. 55–61.

TUCKER, MARCIA (April 9–May 31, 1970). *Robert Morris,* exhibition catalogue (New York: Whitney Museum of American Art).

VENET, BERNAR (April 5–May 18, 1970). *Meta-Mathematik, Fotos, Schrift,* exhibition catalogue (Krefeld, West Germany: Museum Haus Lange).

VENTURI, LIONELLO (1936). *History of Art Criticism* (New York: E. P. Dutton, 1964).

WARHOL, ANDY; KÖNIG, KASPER; HULTÉN, PONTUS; and GRANATH, OLLE (eds.) (February–March, 1968). *Andy Warhol,* exhibition catalogue (Stockholm: Moderna Museet, 2nd ed., 1969).

WEITZ, MORRIS (May 14, 1970). "The Concept of Style in Art History," paper given at the University of Delaware Symposium concerning The Philosophy and History of Art (to be published).

WÖLFFLIN, HEINRICH (1915). *Principles of Art History: The Problem of the Development of Style in Later Art*, translated by M. D. Hottinger (New York: Dover Publications, 1932).

WORRINGER, WILHELM ROBERT (1908). *Abstraction and Empathy*, translated by Michael Bullock (New York: International University Press, 1963).

Index